HERE AND HEREAFTER

HERE AND HEREAFTER

By request, more information on
life in the Spirit World from

Monsignor Robert Hugh Benson

Recorded by

Anthony Borgia

© Tony Ortzen

First published 1958
This edition 2020

Published by
Saturday Night Press Publications
England

snppbooks@gmail.com
www.snppbooks.com

ISBN 978-1-908421-46-3

www.snppbooks.com

Cover design: *Ann Harrison at Saturday Night Press:* © *own
photograph 'Mediterranean blue, 1978.'*

CONTENTS

Preface

Since the first of our scripts was published there has been a steady stream of letters from readers all over the world, each of them showing an immense interest in psychic science and, in particular, in the subject matter of the scripts themselves. So much so, indeed, that our readers have constantly asked for still more information upon this important subject.

In compiling the scripts, our communicator's chief problem, he has always said, is not so much what to say, but what to omit, since, he says regretfully, with the limitations of space it is impossible, in describing the life and people of so vast a place as the spirit world 'to get a quart into a pint pot'.

It is inevitable therefore, that much interesting matter should be omitted altogether or have but fugitive reference to it. With this in mind, but chiefly in view of the great number of requests for additional information, our communicator has dictated this present volume, which was completed in 1957, and I use the word dictated in its literal sense. As with the previous scripts, I received the dictation by means of clairaudience. Should this fail, as at times it is almost inevitable that it should, then direct inspiration was resorted to—it mattered not which, for both were equally effective.

For my part, every care was exercised to ensure absolute accuracy and authenticity, and to this end I was anxious that the scripts should have some sort of independent verification, at least, my share of them. This I was able to do through the services of a non-professional trance-medium of the highest integrity, during the course of twice-weekly circle-sittings. I was thus able to talk directly to the communicator, who gave me his verbal assurance independently that I had taken down correctly all he had to say.

Interested readers may be wishful to know, perhaps, how the communicator views the results of his achievement regarding the previous books and their penetration into many lands. He says with warm appreciation: 'I am delighted with the results that have far exceeded my expectation.'

A voluminous, world-wide correspondence has itself been a 'revelation', our readers being folk of all ages, from a youthful 20 to an equally youthful 80 years of age. Throughout all the letters, I have been almost overwhelmed by the writers' many expressions of appreciation and gratitude, of cordiality and warmth. *Life in the World Unseen*,' writes one minister of the Church, 'has given me much inspiration. Thank you most sincerely.' And the wife of a clergyman wrote to say: 'I have read your indescribably lovely book through twice already, and hope to read it many times more.' It is not surprising, therefore, that our communicator should have feelings of justifiable gratification.

Here and Hereafter is, in fact, complete in itself, and while it is not a sequel to the two previous books, it bears a thematic relationship to them by responding to our readers' oft-repeated entreaties (in the words of Goethe) for 'light, more light'.

A. B.

Introduction

It seems incredible that the organised body known, collectively, as 'the Church', while speaking repeatedly and familiarly of heaven, confesses to knowing nothing whatever about that future state. (A clergyman once wrote to me that nine-tenths of his congregation did not believe in a hereafter at all.)

On the other hand, one Church in particular claims to know a good deal about hell, one of its most important features being that once a person has got into it, there is no getting out of it. One's residence there is for all eternity. A priest of this Church was once asked if he really believed in hell. 'Oh, yes,' he replied, 'but I don't believe anyone ever goes there!'

The Church has made the hereafter into a place of mystery, and the whole subject of a future state has been wrapped round with a mantle of religiosity, until people have come to look upon it with fear, with awe, with scepticism, with ridicule, with horror, and with a variety of other emotions according to their several temperaments or upbringings.

Death can come to a person slowly or rapidly, but it must inevitably come sooner or later. There is no dodging it. It has been going on since life began. Would it not be a relief to many minds, then, if they knew something, even if only a little, about the possible or probable state of their being after they have made the change from this life to the next? In other words, what sort of place is the next world? The only way to find out is to ask someone who lives there, and to record what is said. And the latter is precisely what has been done in this present volume as in the two that have preceded it.

It is again necessary to say that I first came to know the communicator of this book, Monsignor Robert Hugh Benson, many years ago. A son of Edward White Benson, former Archbishop of Canterbury, he was then at the summit of his fame both as author and preacher.

By telling others, who are still on earth, of his experiences in the spirit world, he will have attained more than his purpose if he is able to cast out of people's minds the fear of death and the hereafter.

Anthony Borgia

I

THE THRESHOLD

When we first began to set down[1] the joint experiences of Edwin, Ruth, and myself of our life in the spirit world, I was told that there would be some who would take exception to what I had to say upon one particular incident or another. Indeed, that was almost bound to happen among thinking people whose eye I should be fortunate enough to catch.

The thoughts of many persons still upon earth have come to us here in the spirit world as a consequence of the narration of those experiences.

Some there are who have thought to themselves, and, indeed, voiced the opinion to their friends, that the descriptions I have given of the spirit world, or rather, of that part of it with which I am acquainted, are almost too good to be true. An ideal state, they would say, that is too wonderful to exist in actual fact. The picture I have painted, they would continue, is an imaginative one, and has no existence outside the imagination.

Now, that attitude of mind is not confined to the earth. People who are newly arrived in the spirit world express exactly the same opinion upon thousands of occasions. They simply cannot realise the concrete existence of all the wonders and beauties and marvels that they see around them. At least, they cannot do so at first. When they do realise it, their joy is supreme.

1. *Life in the World Unseen* and *More about Life in the World Unseen*

So that, if seeing these entrancing things brings with it an initial and temporary disbelief, then it is not surprising that mere descriptions of them should engender something of a similar disbelief among people still upon earth.

But the validity of my descriptions still remains, whatever adverse opinion or disagreement may be expressed upon them. I cannot alter the truth. What Edwin, Ruth, and I have seen, millions of other folk also have seen, and are still seeing—and enjoying. We would not have one tiny fragment of these conditions altered. They are our life, and they afford us the greatest satisfaction and happiness. When the time comes for any one of us to depart for realms higher above us in spiritual progression, we shall never for a single instant regret the period we have passed in these realms. They will always remain a fragrant and happy memory; and it will always be permissible for us to return to these realms whenever we so wish.

There is an enormous number of people throughout the entire earth that prefers to leave the whole subject of an 'afterlife' alone. These people regard it as an unhealthy subject and treat the very thought of 'death' as morbid. If such people were truly honest with themselves, they would admit that such a state of mind merely increases their fear of 'death' and the 'hereafter', instead of reducing it. They believe that by sweeping the question completely from their minds they will also have dismissed the real fear that so many people have—an instinct, they would say, of self-preservation. Others who are more fortunate and who have no such fears, will divide the unseen world into two principal departments, namely, a place where the wicked will go when they leave the earth, and a place where the not-so-wicked—in which category they would, perhaps, place themselves—will eventually find themselves.

The average earth-dweller has no notion what kind of place 'the next world' can possibly be, usually because he has not given much thought to the matter. How those very same people regret their indifference when they eventually arrive here in the spirit world! 'Why,' they cry, 'were we not told about this before we came here?'

Now, all this arises from the fact that the average person does not know of what he himself is composed. He knows he has a physical body, of course. There are not many who can easily forget it! But leaving the earth in the common act of 'dying' is a perfectly natural and normal process, which has been going on continuously, without intermission, for thousands upon thousands of earthly years.

Man will proudly point to the vast achievements that these passing centuries have seen. He will tell you of the world-shaking discoveries he has made and remind you of the countless inventions for the greater happiness and well-being of man on earth. He will tell you how 'civilised' he has become by comparison with his ancestors of medieval times. He will tell you that he has exact knowledge of this or that, and that many years and vast sums of money have been spent in acquiring that knowledge. But officially, man has neglected the most important study of all—the study of himself, and, arising from it, the study of his ultimate destination when, after his very, very brief span of life on earth, the time comes for him to leave it at 'death' and to journey forth—where?

It is commonly understood that man is composed of body, soul, and spirit. The physical body he is fairly conversant with, but what of the soul and spirit? Of these two, man knows little indeed. What he does not realise is that he is a spirit, first, last, and always. The physical body is merely a vehicle for his spirit body upon his journey through his earthly life.

The mind belongs to the spirit body. Every human experience, every thought, word, and deed, that go to make up the sum of earthly human experience is infallibly and ineradicably recorded upon what is called the subconscious mind through the agency of the physical brain, and when the time comes for man to leave the earth, he discards the physical body for ever, leaves it behind him upon the earth, and passes into the realms of the spirit world. His spirit body he will find is a counterpart of the earthly body he has just left behind him. He will then find that what he called the subconscious mind when he was incarnate has now assumed its rightful place in his new scheme of existence. And it is not long before it begins to show its particular attributes to its owner. By its principal ability of ineffaceable and infallible recording, this mind reveals itself as a complete and perfect chronicle of its owner's life upon earth.

The revelations, therefore, that are attendant upon the person newly arrived in the spirit world can be sufficiently startling.

It is customary among certain minds of the earth to regard the spirit world and its inhabitants as vague and shadowy, extremely unsubstantial and speculative. These same minds regard the dwellers in spirit lands as a class of sub-human beings who are immeasurably worse off than themselves simply because they are 'dead'. To be upon earth is normal, sound, and healthy, and infinitely to be preferred. To be 'dead' is unfortunate—but, of course, inevitable—very unhealthy, and anything but normal. The 'dead' are much to be pitied because they are not alive on earth. This line of thought tends to place an undue importance upon the earthly life and upon the physical body of man. It is as though it were only at the point of 'death' that man takes upon himself any spiritual nature, whereas, in truth, that spiritual nature has been present within him since the moment of his drawing his first breath upon earth.

The whole process of leaving the earth—of dying— is a perfectly natural one. It is merely the operation of a natural law. But for thousands of years the generality of people have lived in entire ignorance of the truth of 'dying' and of the 'hereafter'. And in this, as in so many cases, ignorance, or lack of knowledge, means fear. It is fear of the future following upon 'death' that has surrounded the act of transition with so many mournful and morbid solemnities and doleful trappings.

Sorrow is but natural in human hearts at the parting of loved ones and in their removal from physical sight, but sorrow is aggravated and increased by the lack of knowledge of what precisely has taken place. Orthodox religion is largely responsible for this state of affairs. The one who is mourned has gone to an unknown land where, presumably, an omnipotent God reigns supreme, ready to mete out judgment to all who enter that world. It behoves us, therefore, orthodoxy would urge in effect, that we should do all that we can to placate this Great Judge, that He may deal mercifully with our departed brother. Such a situation, it would be further urged, is no time for anything but the gravest demeanour, the most solemn behaviour.

And how does the departed soul view all these adjuncts of 'death'? Sometimes with disgust, sometimes with amazement at their stupidity, sometimes, and especially with those whose sense of humour is well-developed, with undisguised mirth!

And what of all the paraphernalia of 'death'? Has it

availed the departed soul anything? No, nothing. Black garments, drawn blinds, ponderous solemnity, hushed voices, and countenances of exaggerated gloom are utterly worthless to help the soul upon its way. Indeed, the reverse can, in many cases, be the result. But of that I will speak to you later. For the moment I wish to show you that 'dying' is the operation of a simple and natural law; that it is healthy and normal to consider the subject, and discuss it, and find out all about it.

Surely the greatest stimulus to enquiry should be occasioned by the thought that every single soul born upon earth must, at some time or another, face the death of his physical body. Let us begin, then by briefly sketching the operation of physical death.

The spirit body exactly coincides with the physical body, and during waking hours the two are inseparable. When sleep takes place the spirit body withdraws from the physical body, but the former is attached to the latter by a magnetic cord. I call it a magnetic cord for want of a better name. It is a veritable lifeline. Its elasticity is enormous, since the spirit body can travel either throughout the earth during sleeping hours, or throughout the spirit world subject to special conditions and limitations. However vast the distance between the sleeping physical body and the temporarily released spirit body, the magnetic cord can span the distance easily and perfectly and without any diminution of its active agency, which is to sustain life in the earthly body. The lifeline will, as its length increases, become exceedingly fine and almost hair-like in appearance.

Just so long as the magnetic cord is joined to the earthly body, just so long will earthly life remain in the physical body. But the moment that dissolution takes place the lifeline is severed, the spirit is free to live in its own element, while the physical body will decay in the manner which is perfectly familiar to you upon earth.

The death of the physical body, then, is simply the severance of the magnetic cord, and as far as the physical body is concerned it is closely akin to ordinary sleep. There does not seem anything very dreadful about this straightforward process if a little thought is given to it.

I have already spoken to you concerning my own passage to this world of the spirit. It was easy and comfortable, and I was certainly not aware of any distress when the actual moment arrived for the magnetic cord to break from my physical body. As far as I was concerned there was no shock or struggle, no unpleasant circumstances of any description.

Since my own advent into spirit lands, I have talked with many friends upon this matter, and not one of them was aware by any internal or external incident that their magnetic cord had parted from their physical bodies. In this respect the actual process of dissolution is painless. Whatever suffering is endured by the person whose transition is imminent, is purely physical. That is to say, it is the cause of physical death, from disease, for example, or accident, that may bring pain and not the actual death itself. If doctors can relieve the pain, and there is no reason why in all cases they should not, then the whole course of dissolution would be entirely painless. Why should the severance of the magnetic cord be a painful operation? If it were, it would surely suggest that there were some fault in the heavenly scheme of things. But there is no fault, and 'death' is painless.

And now, what happens next? Just this: the person who has just passed into spirit lands goes to his own *self-appointed place.*

At the very outset, this would seem to suggest that I have overlooked what is known as 'judgment', where every man shall be judged according to his merits and rewarded or condemned—received into heaven, or sent to hell.

No, I have not overlooked it, because there is no such thing as being judged at any time, either by the Father of the Universe or by any single soul that lives in the spirit world. There is no Judgment Day.

Man, himself, is his own judge. His thoughts, his words, and his deeds, registered upon his mind, are his only judge, and according to how his earthly life has been lived, so will his place be in these lands of the spirit world. This is another natural law, and like all the laws of the spirit world, perfect in its operation. It requires no interpreters of it, no exponents of it. It is self-acting and incorruptible and, what is most important, it is impartial and infallible.

The old idea of a Recording Angel, whose especial function is to inscribe in a great book all our good deeds and all our bad deeds, is poetic enough, but completely wrong. We do our own recording for ourselves, and this is one instance at least when we speak truly! We cannot hide our bad deeds, but, also, we cannot conceal our good deeds. I am using the word deeds in a general sense.

What really counts in our earthly lives is the motive behind our deeds. Our motives may be of the highest, but the actual deed may have a poor external appearance. And the reverse is equally true. For example, a man may give vast sums of money for some charitable purpose with the sole thought of persona publicity and self-aggrandisement. While the gift itself may do great good to those upon whom it is bestowed, the motive behind the gift will not be to the giver's spiritual advantage. But if this same donor were to perform a small service to another person in difficulty or similar circumstances, all unwitnessed by a third party, and with the sole intention of helping a fellow mortal in distress, such unobtrusive and stealthy service brings a rich reward to him who performs it. It is motive, always, that counts.

The richest services are most often those that are performed without a fanfare of trumpets. So many of us here in the spirit world are surprised when we discover that some small service that we have done— and immediately afterwards forgotten has helped us in our spiritual progression to an extent that we should scarcely have thought possible. But here we see things in their proper light, that is, in their true light, because they are registered within ourselves in their true light.

So you see, we need no one to condemn us. No one could condemn us more strictly, more exactly, more truly and efficiently than we do ourselves. When we come to the spirit world at our dissolution we thus find ourselves in the precise environment for which we have fitted ourselves. That environment may be one of darkness or of light, or it may be one of gloomy greyness. But wherever it may be, we have ourselves to thank, or blame for it.

But, you will naturally ask, having in mind certain orthodox religious teachings on the subject, are those who dwell in greyness or darkness confined to those regions for all eternity? No, no! Never for all eternity. They will remain there for just so long as they wish. Indeed, some of them have lived in the dark realms for thousands of years, but thousands of years is not eternity, although it may seem like it sometimes to some of the inhabitants of those regions. But every soul so situated in darkness is free to terminate his sojourn there whenever he sees fit. The choice rests with himself.

If the denizens of the darker regions show no aptitude towards spiritual progression and so lifting themselves out of the darkness, then they will remain where they are. No one forces them to stay there. They themselves elect to do so.

The instant that one of the unhappy inhabitants shows the most minute tendency to lift himself out of the sad conditions of those dark realms, such tendency becomes a wish that others higher up can see, and every help is given to that soul to place his feet firmly and strongly upon the upward path of progression. That pathway may be steep and difficult, but neither so steep nor difficult but that some one cannot help him to surmount all the obstacles upon the way. This is spiritual progression in the fullest sense of the word. It is open to all.

We in this beautiful realm of light are all working for our spiritual advancement. It is not restricted to those who live in the dark regions. The people who inhabit the magnificent spheres above this wherein I dwell, are all moving forward and upward in their triumphant progressional march. It never ceases, and spiritual progress is the birth-right of every single soul.

The whole crude conception of being damned for all eternity arises from a totally wrong conception of the Father of the Universe, a grotesque conception that has found its supporters throughout the centuries, and that has, in consequence, put fear into the hearts of mankind. It is a man-made belief without the slightest foundation in fact. And it is not long before a newcomer to the spirit world finds out that the whole idea of eternal damnation is an utterly impossible one.

And now, here is something that Edwin, Ruth, and I

discovered early in our joint endeavours. When newly-arrived persons, who obviously could never qualify for eternal damnation, are told that such a thing does not, never did, or ever will exist, they exhibit an immensely strong sense of relief.

They usually explain that this feeling of relief is not, as it were on their own behalf, but partly on behalf of all those others less fortunate than themselves, and partly from the far-reaching possibilities and prospects that this absence of eternal damnation suggests to their minds.

They see at once that the whole spirit world lies before them in equal right with their fellow human beings, and that the God of whom they were always rather frightened when on earth is a Father of unlimited and illimitable benevolence, and One, moreover, who could never breathe vengeance upon any one of His children. That in itself is an illuminating discovery which is of great service to the newcomer to spirit lands, since it at once opens his mind to the truth.

A moment ago, I told you that the person who has just passed into the spirit world goes to his own self-appointed place, but you hear of individuals, who are new arrivals, wandering about aimlessly, apparently lost, and who do not seem to know what has befallen them. Can it be that they do not know that they have passed on?

Such is the state of spiritual enlightenment of the earth that in many cases these folk are completely unaware that they have 'died'. That means simply that they have never ceased to live; there has been an unbroken continuity of life for them, as indeed there is for all of us. This situation frequently arises among people who pass into the spirit world suddenly and perhaps without warning. Their lack of knowledge of conditions existing in the spirit world produces this state of bewilderment, and if there is added to that ignorance also the fact that, during their earthly life, they never gave any heed to a future life in the spirit world, then their situation becomes a doubly unhappy one. But there is in the spirit world a vast organization of all its immense resources, and it must not be thought that these bewildered souls are left to shift for themselves. They are soon taken in hand by others long resident in spirit lands—as you judge time—who devote their spirit lives to such work. Edwin, Ruth and I have for years been engaged upon this identical work, so that I can speak from particular experience.

Our task is often a difficult one because it is not always easy for the soul to grasp what has happened. The mental equipment of the individual may cause a reluctance to accept the truth. On the other hand, those who are mentally alert will soon see for themselves the exact situation.

If only knowledge of the laws and conditions of spirit life were universally diffused throughout the earth world, what a wealth of difference it would make to each soul as he came to reside in these lands.

Was anyone ever so ill-equipped for a journey as is the average person for the journey into these spirit lands?

It is a journey that all, all must take, and how many even bother to think about it during their earthly life?

This voyage is inevitable, without failure, but so many thousands of people are perfectly content to dismiss from their minds all thought of it until the times comes to take it. Many have no chance even at the last moment to think about it, so sudden is their transition.

How many people living on earth would be foolish

enough to undertake a journey with their eyes blindfolded, not knowing how far they were travelling, or whence, or to what conditions of living? Yet so many are willing to embark upon the first great voyage of their lives in absolute ignorance of all these factors. We in the spirit world are constantly seeing these bewildered souls arriving, and we do our best for them. We have then no need to chide them, for they are the first to blame themselves. And as often as not, they do so in good round terms!

I think if one were asked what was the most common mental state in which the majority of people arrive in the spirit world, I should be disposed to reply from a fairly extensive experience, that they arrive in a state of bewilderment and complete ignorance of the fact that they have passed from the earth world.

Speaking for myself, I was more fortunate than a great many, for I did know what was happening from my slight acquaintance with psychic matters. Even slender knowledge is of help in such cases, and I was glad of it then.

Relatives and friends, who have passed on before us, can help in such extremities, and they frequently do so. But some mutual interest must exist first, even if it does not reach to the state of affectionate regard. Affection is the great linking force in the spirit world. Without it a gulf comes between people. If you have never given a thought while you are on earth to those who have passed into the spirit world before you, or otherwise shown any friendly interest in your 'deceased' family and friends, there is not much incentive or encouragement for such relatives and friends to display any concern on your behalf. Mutual interest, affection, or regard provide the active living link between individuals. Without them a gulf develops, and each and all of the parties will become detached and wander away to other interests and attachments.

The circumstances in which a person can pass into the spirit world vary so enormously with individual cases that it would be next to impossible to describe all of them to you. It would take volumes to do so. I can only therefore, speak to you in general terms. These circumstances vary not only from the personal point of view, but the very state of life upon earth will help to diversify the actual transitions.

In ancient days great plagues would send thousands of souls into spirit lands in most distressing conditions. In modern times one has no need to point to the devastating wars that cast people loose into the spirit world with shocking suddenness. In many cases such sudden dissolution is a great shock to the spirit body undergoing it. But here again the spirit world has risen to every contingency. Homes of rest exist here especially for the treatment of people who have undergone a sudden transition.

The shock which is sustained is not exactly the same as would be the case of a shock merely to the physical body, though it is nearly enough like it for your understanding. But the results can be entirely dissimilar. In the rest homes of the spirit world a cure is certain to be brought about without any possibility of doubt, and upon full recovery the victim of the shock is not one whit the worse for the experience. The memory of it remains, though only perhaps dimly, without any recurring reactions upon the mind of an unpleasant nature. And there are no resulting fears implanted in the mind such as would be the case with the physical body.

Many people have passed into the spirit world in what the earth would call a dreadful manner—and dreadful it might be in earthly eyes—yet when they have come to tell me about their rapid transition, their 'sudden death', they have treated the whole episode with a light heart, and often are perfectly ready to joke about the matter. Indeed, I have heard friends remark that they entered the spirit world in a most undignified manner! And that, I think, demonstrates the precise difference in the way in which 'death' is regarded by us here in the spirit world and by you still upon earth. Here we view things in their proper perspective, while ignorance has distorted things so much upon earth. The 'death' of the physical body is a tragedy to the earth world. To the spirit world it is the operation of a natural law unattended by any mournful solemnities. While the physical body is being consigned to its earthly abode accompanied by all the ceremonial trappings and dismal black habiliments of minister and mourners, the spirit body containing the real and everlasting substance of personality has gone to its proper abode in the spirit world.

In these realms we receive our friends amid great rejoicings. Another friend has come to join us. We wear no black, we do not recite long gloomy prayers or perform harrowing ceremonies. Nor do we have a reception committee of 'angels', as many people are disposed to imagine is, or ought to be, the case. We merely behave in a normal rational human manner as one would expect from normal rational human beings. We are not pontifically welcomed among the 'elect'. We are not made free citizens of these realms because we have been 'saved' through believing in some strange, obscure theological creed. We are not here because we have been 'redeemed' through the offices of another. We are here solely because we have, by our lives on earth or by our progress in the spirit world, earned the right to call ourselves citizens of these realms. We are here

because no one can keep us out! Once we have the right
to be here, no one can gainsay that right, no one can
dispute it, no one *would* dispute it even if he could.

Many people here regard their advent into spirit
lands as their second birth, and they keep up the
celebration of the second birthday with a deal more
vigour than they ever did their birthday on earth.

In speaking of the magnetic cord, I mentioned that
during sleep the spirit body sometimes visits other
places either on earth or in the spirit world. It is not
everyone, however, that travels during sleeping hours.
It depends entirely upon individual circumstances.
When no visiting takes place the spirit body is content
merely to linger in the vicinity of the sleeping physical
body until such time as the resting period is ended.
With some people a desire to visit other parts of the
earth is uppermost in the mind of the sleeper. The
reason for doing so will vary according to his tastes or
circumstances.

Visits to the spirit world are frequently made for
some more important purpose, because there is so much
useful work that can be done upon such visits.

These visits are usually made by people who are
conversant with spirit truths, and who are eager to add
to their knowledge. While these visitations are in
progress they can meet and converse with such of their
relatives and friends who have passed into spirit lands
before them. Old relationships are renewed; indeed, it
would be more accurate to say that they are continued
since they have not been interrupted. The visitor can
gain useful help and guidance upon his earthly affairs
from people who, from their superior position in the
spirit world, are able to offer assistance.

How often have you heard people on earth remark
that they will 'sleep on it' when they are confronted

with some problem that needs solution? Invariably the morning brings to their problem the answer that they have sought. And in the great majority of cases the solution has been afforded them after they have held a consultation with their friends in the spirit world during their sleeping hours. Most people have some problem or another that is upon their minds, but not all of them come here during sleep for guidance in material matters.

Hundreds of individuals, who are in active communication with the spirit world, come to us here when they retire to rest upon earth, and with their knowledge of the laws of the spirit world they can give *us* material help of no small consideration in a variety of ways. They become temporarily one of our community of friends, enjoy the delights of these realms, enter into our affairs as one of us—as they will be permanently one day—work with us, indulge in our recreations, and so forward their own spiritual progression in a score of different ways.

Imagine the rejoicing when regular visitors to our realms at length come to take up their permanent abode with us. The information and knowledge that they have been accumulating during the years, but which, during their waking hours on earth, they will scarcely recollect, will now take their place in their minds and memories as useful experiences. These experiences will establish the continuity of their existence since their birth on earth, instead of transplanting them into the spirit world with the feeling that they must start life anew.

Many souls who are mourning those who have passed into the spirit world, leaving sad hearts behind them, can bring comfort and consolation to themselves even if only in a limited degree, by nightly visitations and meetings in the spirit world with those whom they mourn. Many a soul so afflicted has arisen from his bed in the morning with an unaccountable feeling that comfort has come to him in some mysterious fashion. This means of lessening the distress of separation is but another instance of the perfection of the dispensation that is the very foundation upon which the whole spirit world is built and upheld.

But such means of consolation is only a by-product, if one can so term it, of that larger knowledge of spirit truths. It is only a very limited means to an end, since it merely provides a rather unsubstantial antidote to acute sorrow and sadness. While it will reduce both the sorrow and sadness it does not provide the certain knowledge that all is well with the one who is being mourned. Active communication will alone provide that, and it is infinitely to be preferred to any presentiments in the matter.

The spirit world disapproves of mourning in every shape and form. Genuine, heartfelt sorrow is a human emotion that none of us is secure from, but so much mourning is spurious. Here we can see just what is taking place in the minds of the mourners. Mourning as a rule is utterly selfish, because people are not sorry for the soul who has passed on except in so far as it is thought that he is now infinitely worse off 'dead'. The great majority of people are *sorry for themselves* at the physical separation, not happy and glad that their friend has gone to a greater, grander, more beautiful life. Of course, I am now speaking of those who are destined for the realms of light. With those whose destination here is in the realms of darkness we are not treating at the moment.

Even where the sorrow is perfectly genuine and inspired by true affection, every effort should be made to curb it. The soul newly arrived in spirit lands will feel the determined drag of the thoughts of those who are left behind, unless those thoughts are constructive thoughts for the present and future wellbeing of the friend who has gone.

Thoughts of the wrong kind will draw the soul back like a magnet and prevent it from making a steady and natural transition into its proper sphere. It is no exaggeration to say that it would be immeasurably better, things being what they are upon earth, if mourners on earth were to pass into a complete state of physical insensibility for some days after the passing of a friend into the spirit world. There would then be no danger of the thoughts of others circumscribing the actions of the newly-departed soul.

The strong attachment to the physical body that exists in the minds of so many people would be largely broken down if those same people were to become fully acquainted with spirit truths.

Our friends who are in communication with us and who have knowledge of the facts of life in the spirit world, have given to the physical body *its* proper position in relation to *their* life on earth and their life *after* in the spirit world. They know that their physical body is a vehicle for their spirit body while upon earth. When the time comes for them to leave the earth world, and with it their earthly body, the latter is treated as something that is for ever done with. It has become utterly useless to them. It has been cast off—and our friends are never sorry to cast it off! What then becomes of it they are not the least bit concerned. They have no reverence for it. But so many people enshroud this cast-off body with a holy solemnity to which it is not entitled. The 'dead', it would be asserted, should have a proper respect paid to them; the 'dead' body should be similarly respected.

Let us put the matter in another light. Who is there upon earth who has any deep respect and reverence for some old, useless, worn-out, shabby garment? It is finished and done with. Away with it, and let us see no more of it. In the spirit world we have a new garment, fresh and lovely; it fits us perfectly, and it seems to our eyes faultless in form, colour and mode. It suits us now as no other garment possibly could. We have fashioned it ourselves from imperishable material, and by comparison with it our earthly garment was dull, drab, and dreary in colour, coarse in texture, ill-fitting, perhaps, in places, and although it served its purpose among surroundings that comported with it, we have now something infinitely better. In some such words would we describe our spirit attitude to the physical body that is 'dead'.

Old customs and old traditions, though they may be themselves worthless, take a deal of killing. It has become the custom to surround the disposal of the physical body after 'death' with melancholy rites, begotten of the general disposition of regarding transition, from the earthly point of view, as a major disaster. But there are other and greater reasons for wishing that 'funeral rites' were either considerably modified or entirely abolished in their present form upon earth.

From the moment of passing until the physical body is finally committed to the earth, and frequently for some time afterwards, the thoughts of the mourners are concentrated in sorrow upon the departed one. The various performances that comprise the 'last rites' add force to this sorrow, enhance it, and give it greater directive power. Where this feeling of sorrow is genuine it will unfailingly reach the recently departed soul.

The spirit body may take some days of your time before it becomes completely separated from the earthly body, and it may be hindered very much by the combined thoughts of the sorrowers who are participants in the dismal rites. Instead of departing from the earthly sphere, the discarnate one will be attracted to the scene of obsequial activities, and more than likely will be saddened himself by what he is witnessing and by the sorrow of those he has left behind. He will feel a heavy weight within him of the separation that has come about, and perhaps being ignorant of what has befallen him, he will be doubly distressed, and even trebly distressed by the fact that he speaks to his friends, but they cannot hear him. And how great a difference a little knowledge would make!

What we in the spirit world, who are actively associated with newly-arrived people, would like to see is the complete abolition of all attendance at burial grounds and similar places of all relatives and friends, leaving the physical body to be disposed of in a hygienic manner by those who are properly constituted to do so, and entirely unattended by anyone else. If it is felt that a religious service is right and becoming, by all means let there be one, but wholly purged of all erroneous doctrines and beliefs concerning the afterlife. No gloomy dwelling upon inappropriate themes from the minds of writers of hundreds of years ago. *Dies iree, dies ilia* has most emphatically no place in the spirit world, and still less has the outrageous idea embodied in the customary prayers, of asking for 'eternal rest' to be granted to the departed soul. We shudder at the very thought of what our state in the spirit world would be if the prayers of others had been granted! The very thought of doing positively nothing but 'rest' for all eternity fills us all with horror at such a 'soul-destroying' prospect. If it were possible to destroy the soul, one would be disposed to imagine that this would be the quickest and easiest way of doing it!

Let there be prayers for the departed one, by all means, but let them be free from all suggestion of gloom and doom. The minds of those present want to be elevated, not depressed, and nothing could be more depressing than the calamitous forebodings that are voiced in so many of the prayers on these occasions.

The departed one has not gone to another world to be marched in front of a stern Judge, a Judge, moreover, not so stern and unrelenting but that our lamentations will not bring some mitigation in the sentence to be pronounced. Indeed, the prayers should be brief and very much to the point. And here I can again speak from particular personal experience.

Let the prayers be addressed to the Father of us all, that help may be sent to the soul who has passed on, and that the Father will also aid those who are offering their ministrations to the newly-arrived one. We need divine assistance in our work just as do you upon earth, and often are our powers taxed to their utmost when we come to aid those who are making their advent into spirit lands as permanent residents. Long recitations from the psalmists, however beautiful may be their theme, are perfectly useless to us and to the newcomer we are helping. They produce no effect whatever upon the endeavours we are making.

A short prayer, efficiently directed, asking for help, will bring an instantaneous answer. That response will be invisible to you on earth, but to us here it means a downpouring of light and power that we most need for the case in hand. Pray that the soul may soon receive the light of understanding of the new situation in which he finds himself, if he is entirely ignorant of spirit truths, and that he may be happy and contented in the life upon which he has just embarked.

We have found by experience that where prayers are

offered such as I have suggested in bare outline to you, we are enabled to carry on our work in the easiest, most effective, and most straightforward fashion.

It may be objected that on such occasions it is next to impossible to be anything but utterly downcast, and that prayers, to a certain extent, must be in the same minor key; that anything approaching lightness of heart is out of the question, not only from the situation itself, but in respect for the feelings of others. There is a very simple remedy for this: a knowledge of spirit truths.

Consider the matter thus. In most cases the mourners are lamenting the departure of someone for a destination that is unknown to them—and, they would say, that is unknowable. They are a little frightened, not necessarily for their departed friend, but for themselves when their own time should come, because—by what they are witnessing—they are forcibly reminded of what inevitably lies before them and before all men.

Unfortunately, their knowledge is limited strictly to the fact of the death of the physical body. After that has taken place, what happens? They know not—and it scarcely bears thinking about, because that sort of thing is unhealthy and morbid. But the fear remains just the same, so that in the very presence of 'death' they are apprehensive. And being apprehensive they have no time for being anything else. The mournful obsequies are therefore completely in tune with their present emotion. They feel solemn, and diffident, and somewhat cowed, but they have the great consolation of knowing that they are alive while their friend is 'dead'.

Now transitions have been taking place since the world began thousands of centuries ago, but mankind in general is content to remain in ignorance of what is to happen to him when he leaves the earth for the spirit world. He either asserts that it is impossible to know, or else he prefers to abide in his ignorance. And yet if he had but the knowledge of even the simple facts such as I have detailed to you, what a wealth of difference it would make to his mind. It would drive out that dreadful fear of the unknown 'hereafter' which can be, and is, such a crushing nightmare to sensitive minds.

I am disposed to believe that not only is it fear of the unknown that distresses people, but also the thought that physical dissolution is a painful process. A study of the facts and truths of life in the spirit world is the best antidote—indeed, it is the only antidote—for fears such as I have mentioned. Great faith may go a long way, but faith can never take the place of facts. And then instead of giving the departing soul a harrowing, sorrowful send-off, with a knowledge of the truth the same soul could be given all the help he needs in a powerful, bright and happy 'God-speed'.

It is unquestionably a bad practice, too, to frequent burial grounds for the purpose of attending to the upkeep of graves and tombs. It is not difficult to see why this should be so in the light of what I have told you upon the subject in general. Such places will start a train of depressing thoughts concentrated upon the one whose grave is being visited. The latter will be the recipient of such sorrowful thoughts as both the place and the circumstances are bound to engender, and these thoughts will exert a drawing influence upon certain types of mentalities that is extremely difficult to resist. The soul will be unable to combat the seemingly irresistible urge to visit the place whence the thoughts are coming, which in this case is the worst of all places—the tomb of the cast-off physical body. We do our best to ward off such thoughts, as it were, but we cannot go beyond certain limits, and where the person insists upon exercising his free will and wishes to be left to decide for himself in the matter, then we are bound to withdraw and allow the soul free passage.

Many people will, however, listen to our reasoning, and so save themselves an infinity of distress and unhappiness. If for no other reason than this, it would be the best thing upon the earth if cemeteries, graveyards, and all the visible and outward appurtenances of burial were entirely abolished. Large numbers of people would then be forced to relinquish what is a thoroughly bad practice from every point of view. It is unhealthy for mundane as well as spiritual reasons and can be the unconscious means of bringing distress to the newly departed individual.

From the fact that a mourner is spending time at the grave, indulging in melancholy thoughts of the soul who has passed on, and contemplating that a few feet of earth are now separating them, and so on, you will infer, in such a case, that the mourner has no acquaintance with spirit truths, or else he would never think that the departed one really lies there himself.

We in the spirit world know that a soul who gradually yields to such melancholy importunities of thought as are being sent out from the earth, knows very little of spirit truths. And being in such case, when a soul returns to the earth and stands in the presence of the mourner and tries to talk to and comfort the one who is left behind, he becomes acutely disturbed in mind when he discovers that his voice cannot be heard on the earth. His words are falling unheeded upon the air. The thoughts of sorrow and despair pass and re-pass in a constant stream until at last both persons become exhausted with the emotional strain. The mourner will eventually leave the graveside, the newly-arrived spirit will return whence he came, and both are filled with inconsolable sadness. The whole performance has done no good whatever; on the contrary, it has had a very bad effect upon both parties. And what is still worse, the episode will be repeated and repeated until we on our side can instil some reason into our distracted friend and show him the futility of the proceedings. Better counsels will eventually prevail, and the visitations to the resting place of the physical body will cease. In the meantime, the soul has passed through a period of untold misery that could have been avoided if only those who were left behind upon earth had possessed themselves of the necessary knowledge of spirit truths.

You can understand that we are not pleased with the wilful stupidity of some earth folk who persist in closing their eyes and ears to the truth, and so causing an enormous amount of misery to friends and relatives who have passed into the spirit world before them. Their blind ignorance in refusing to look at the facts of spiritual truths, their blatant assumption of mental superiority over the whole subject of spirit life, their self-satisfied attachment to their own erroneous views, all these, taken together or individually, have the effect of giving us work to do in the spirit world which a knowledge of the truth would render totally unnecessary. We should then be enabled to carry on with other work than correcting the mistakes of the earth. The earth has, in fact, a completely exaggerated idea of its own cleverness. You need to be resident in the spirit world to see just how foolish mankind upon earth can really be! Here the mistakes are plain for all to see, and we are sometimes amazed at the ignorance displayed.

It must not be supposed that I am claiming infallibility for the people of the spirit world. Far from it. But man, when he is incarnate, has so many opportunities of learning about the life in the spirit world that lies before him. He wilfully passes the chances by with an airy wave of the hand, because he *knows* better. When he comes to the spirit plane of existence he knows better still, and bitterly laments the wasted opportunities of his earthly life. And there are few worse things than remorse. But we can come to the rescue in this as in so many other things, and help the soul to overcome the remorse for his earthly mistakes.

We are certainly not infallible here in the spirit world, but by virtue of our altered state we can see just a little farther ahead than can you who are still incarnate. When we perceive that our friends on earth are about to make some mistake or other that will eventually be to their disadvantage, we are naturally anxious to offer a word of caution or advice, and so save them from the consequences. Alas, man is so often deaf to our promptings, and the false move is made. Eventually, when our friend arrives in the spirit world, he sees the mistakes he has made and how he could have prevented them had he but listened.

Death always seems to the beholder of it to be such a solitary business, as perforce, it must be to some extent. But our help is always at hand, though help comes usually after the severance of the magnetic cord when the spirit body is free from the earthly body. The severance will take place in a perfectly natural manner, just as the leaf will fall from the tree. It is then that the moment comes for us to step in and offer our assistance. I say *offer* assistance because we do not force our services upon anyone. However, in all our experience so far, our offers of help have never been scorned. On the contrary, people are only too glad to leave themselves entirely in our hands.

Incidentally, we three, Edwin, Ruth, and I, have made literally countless friends through the instrumentality of our work. So many of them regard us as the first face upon which they cast their spirit eyes when death had closed their physical eyes. They regarded us then as friends in need, who had come to save them from heaven knows what nameless ordeals, and, if for no other reason than this, our work is repaid a hundredfold by the look of heartfelt relief upon their countenances and by the exuberance of their gratitude as we explain some of the pleasant things that are awaiting them. And never was gratitude more genuine!

The actual process of physical death must be undertaken alone, and in this sense, it is a solitary business. But as soon as the spirit body is free then we can begin.

So far I have been speaking of people who are destined for the bright realms of the spirit world. Equally, assistance is offered to those whose lives on earth have brought them to the dark realms. It is a safe rule to say that no person passing into the spirit world at dissolution does so unattended. There is always *someone* there. But in so many cases we are prevented from giving any help by the spiritual state of the soul we are approaching. In fact, approach becomes impossible, and so we can do nothing but watch the soul depart upon its way into darkness. Naturally, if we can perceive the tiniest glimmer of light issuing from such a soul, we do our best to fan it into something more resembling a flame.

You must know that spirituality means light, literally, with us here in the spirit world. And absence of spirituality means darkness. The soul in the latter case will be just a dark image, the darker it is the more repulsive and hideous, like the life it led upon earth and which is the cause of the blackness. But a dark life may have been relieved in some minute instance by a good action, some kind action, and that will provide the small glimmer of light to which I referred. We can work upon that, as it were, recall it to the mind, and try to show to its owner the difference between this tiny gleam and the rest of its dingy, dark habiliments.

If the soul will listen to reason, then we can make some headway, and so increase the light by the owner's willingness to cleanse the rest of himself. If our words fail to affect the soul in any way, then, perforce, we must let it go upon its way until better thoughts and ideas and wishes come upon the soul in its darkness.

You can understand that this is exacting work for us, in spite of the fact that we do not suffer from physical fatigue. Nevertheless, we cannot continue in such enervating conditions without feeling mentally rather jaded, and so we emerge once more into the light of our own realms. In the meantime, others will take our places, so that no transition is left unattended, no matter where it may be, or in what circumstances, or howsoever caused; whether it be upon land, beneath the land; on the sea or under it, or in the air above the earth. We cannot always achieve our purpose in being present; that is not our fault, but that of the person who has just left his physical body behind him.

A person who is uninstructed in spirit truths can be remarkably obstinate in clinging to his old earthly ideas of what exactly should have taken place when he 'died'. Some may have no views upon the matter whatever, and so may be more amenable to reason and logic. Others may be good folk, but are completely dominated by orthodox religious views, and this type, if anything, is perhaps among the worst of them all to deal with!

There is, over and above these, a certain type of

religious mind that causes us a great deal of trouble, and it is associated with those people upon earth whose religion is of a very crude, elementary description, founded upon a literal interpretation of the scriptures according to their own primitive ideas.

They consider themselves among the 'elect' who are going to be 'gathered up' in some mysterious fashion into the celestial realms, there to be suitably rewarded for their great 'faith'. Their whole religious concept is just as vague in its content and meaning as is this my description of it. The basis is 'faith' in particular scriptural admonitions and precepts and prophecies. They verily believe that their 'creed' will see them through their earthly life into the next world. They believe they will be met by a heavenly host and escorted to their home among the 'elect'.

It never occurs to these people that a life such as they imagine for themselves in heaven would, if realised in all its completeness, become a veritable nightmare to them. They picture themselves spending all eternity in some form of simple worship, which incorporates a vast deal of hymn singing and conversational quotation from the scriptural books.

You can imagine for yourself something of the shock that awaits such souls when they arrive here in the spirit world, to find that they are totally mistaken in the true state of things. At first, they will gravitate to others of their own kind, if we find it impossible, for the moment, to convince them of their errors. At length, their home-made 'heaven' will begin to bore them, until they become thoroughly dissatisfied with their life and surroundings. Then we can step in and introduce them to a normal, natural way of living in the spirit world.

It is strange—is it not my good friend?—that we should have to expend so much labour, undertaken by so many of us here, in explaining to people, ordinary, normal, pleasant, amiable people, the very truth of their being *alive* in every sense of the word!

We have to explain *ourselves* first of all, which may sound stranger still. We have to convince the newly-arrived one that we are not 'ghosts', unsubstantial beings whose sole function in the world is to frighten people. We have become accustomed to being asked the question, 'Who are *you?*'—when we first approach some soul just arrived and in difficulties. And we are obliged to explain that we are very much creatures of 'flesh and blood', and that we have come to help them if they will allow us to do so.

Sometimes the homeliness of our attire and its familiar appearance bring some measure of confidence and assurance to their minds. Our voices, too, seem to be perfectly ordinary and recognisable. For you must know that any suggestion of our appearing as 'celestial beings' would most likely terrify the newcomer and defeat our purpose before we had even commenced to work. Indeed, we are so very matter-of-fact, displaying no suggestion of religious tendencies in our conversation, and speaking to them and treating them as though their present situation were a perfectly commonplace state of affairs—which it is to us, but not to them—that it is not long before an intelligent, receptive mind will grasp the situation in its fullness, and be glad to resign himself to our care.

You will, no doubt, have heard or read of cases of people being 'earthbound' and wondered how this comes about and what 'binds' them to the earth.

In such cases where I have accosted earthbound people, I have always ascertained that the soul so circumstanced was totally unaware of any other state of existence to which he could depart from his present surroundings. He was ignorant of other realms higher or lower than that which he was occupying.

Usually, these unfortunate people are tied to their earthly environment whatever it may be. That attachment may be one of sentiment, where a great affection was entertained for the earthly home, or place of residence, or work. The attraction may be a morbid one, where some misdeed has been committed which draws back the guilty one to the scene of its perpetration. Perhaps this latter is the most familiar to earth people under the designation of 'haunted' places, and many people are puzzled by the fact that in a large number of cases the subject of the 'hauntings' has remained in operation for hundreds of years.

What makes the matter still more puzzling is when the individual who is responsible for the 'hauntings' has all the appearance of being a goodly soul, without any intention of harming or alarming a single person.

What is it that causes him to stay in this spot for these hundreds of years when, presumably, he could be much better employed elsewhere in the spirit world? The answer is that in many instances he is so employed. But you will remember that upon earth there is a familiar saying that it takes all kinds to make a world. Similarly, it takes all kinds to make a spirit world.

Bear that in mind, and remember, too, that a person is exactly the same the moment after he has 'died' as he was the moment before. No magical, instantaneous change takes place either of mind or body. We pass into the spirit world with all our earthly likes and dislikes, all our fancies and foibles, all our idiosyncrasies, and with all our religious errors fast upon us. We are just as we were on earth, though it does not follow in every instance that we will behave just as we did on earth. In the spirit world we have more freedom of expression, and gravitating, as we do, to our own temperamental and spiritual kind, we are not diffident of giving open expression to our thoughts and feelings, and thus presenting, at last, a true picture of ourselves as we really are. Some minds are quick to grasp new ideas and new truths. Some are quick to grasp truth in place of falsehood or untruth. People of this mental calibre soon readjust their views, and so become in harmony with their new life and surroundings. They will 'settle down' for the time being, at least, in their environment.

A great number show no further interest in their old earthly life and mode of living, but will concentrate all their energies upon the larger world that is opening out before them. But there are people who had, while on earth, and still possess now that they are in the spirit world, a sentimental attachment to some place or building. For some reason with which, strictly speaking, they alone are concerned, they show no particular wish to sever that attachment; their interest remains as strong as when they were dwelling therein on earth. They are keenly sensitive of its welfare and vicissitudes, and they take their leisure hours in constantly visiting and revisiting the scene of their former pleasures or activities. At length a time will come when they will grow tired of these journeyings back and forth, with very little actual purpose behind them beyond satisfying a certain curiosity. Then the visits will cease altogether, and the soul will be really free at last. For such ties have no value in them spiritually when the visitor, who is sometimes seen, sometimes only 'felt', and at other times both seen and 'felt', merely returns to satisfy his own interest and curiosity.

To return to the earth with the specific purpose of helping former colleagues or friends is another matter

altogether. Many such people as I have mentioned to
you are simple-minded folk who display a certain
stubbornness on occasion and are consequently deaf to
our suggestions of terminating their 'haunting' of some
particular dwelling on earth. But, in common with us
all, if they choose to exercise their free will to its full
extent, we are powerless to intervene, and they must
pursue their own course. Individuals of this sort are
only partially earthbound. They live in their own proper
realm in the spirit world, making frequent and solitary,
but regular, visits to the place that draws them so
powerfully.

The 'hauntings' of an unpleasant nature where some
crime of violence has been committed, or where some
wrong has remained unredressed, fall into a different
category altogether. In most instances, individuals
remain rooted to the locality. They may still be in the
same frame of mind as upon the original occasion of
their misdeed. They may be consumed with the desire
for vengeance or retribution, or for some form of
violence. So strong will be the concentration of mind
and so powerful the emotion, that the whole incident or
series of incidents will be projected from this harassed
mind in the shape of thought-forms, and these will
assume the precise details, with exact precision, of the
original occurrence. The memory will have recorded the
details faithfully, and the mind will have released
them, and it can go on releasing them with unfailing
exactitude. Any person whose psychic powers are
developed—and sometimes those that are not—will see
what is taking place before them and thereby causing
the 'haunting'.

Occasionally, so powerful is the thought concentration
of the earthbound soul that the whole phenomenon will,
as it were, be forced into the earth world for anyone to
see or hear who should come within range of the

manifestation. That such hauntings should go on for hundreds of years in the same place with similar exactness in each repetition, is not very remarkable when one considers the wide diversity of human minds. The harmless sentimentality of the visitant to old scenes of earthly endeavour can possess a degree of emotional feeling just as strong and binding upon the mind as that of the perpetrator of some crime whose thirst for revenge, shall we say, caused the crime which is now holding him so tenaciously to the earth.

In cases of the latter kind people on earth could afford the spirit world very valuable assistance in relieving of their burden the minds of these tortured souls, or, at least, in giving them some amelioration of their unhappy condition. But so great a number of these occurrences are treated as something to 'investigate', firstly, to see if the alleged haunting is really true, and then, after establishing the fact that something 'queer' does take place, to study the thing with the view, if possible, to seeing what it is all about. After that, long reports are made from eye-witnesses' accounts, the veridical nature of the phenomena is proved, and there the matter rests.

In the meanwhile, the soul who has been the cause of this learned investigation still languishes in his misery. If at the very outset the investigators would interrogate the object of the disturbances and would pray for aid to be sent from the higher realms of the spirit world, not only would unpleasant disturbances be thus terminated, but what is more important, the unhappy cause of them would be helped in his misery and his foot set upon the path of progression.

It is always so much easier, and produces much better results, for people still on earth to tackle these cases in the first instance. The person who is responsible for the haunting is so much nearer the earth and is consequently more easily approached by you than by us here in the spirit world. When he has fully grasped what has happened and what he is doing, then we can take charge of him and lead him away from the environment that is causing the distress.

The mode of one's entry into the spirit world as a permanent resident is the same in every case—through the severance of the magnetic cord, although the physical cause may vary in such ways as are perfectly familiar to you: accident, illness, or old-age. But what may happen to us immediately after the cord is severed may vary infinitely according to the multiplicity of human temperaments which go to make up the populations of the earth, and according to the wide divergence in degrees of spirituality possessed by the new arrivals. Circumstances diversify individual cases to such an extent that it would require many volumes to recount even a part of the experiences of others in the matter of arrival in the spirit world alone. We can only treat the matter in a broad sense.

Among the physical causes of dissolution it would seem that illness would account for the largest number in normal times. What happens to the individual in such cases depends upon several factors.

For example, the length of the illness, and its painfulness or otherwise, and the mental make-up of the individual. Long illness has a tiring effect upon the spirit body—it would be more accurate to say an inhibiting effect upon the spirit body—and when, at last, the physical body is cast off, the spirit body usually goes to one of the numerous halls of rest with which the spirit world is plentifully supplied. There the new resident will pass into a state of pleasant sleep, ultimately to awake fully refreshed and reinvigorated.

The time, as you regard it, taken to achieve this course of treatment varies, of course, to meet individual requirements. With some a comparatively short space of time will serve; with others it might take months of your earthly time.

In my own case, I was ill for only a brief while upon earth. When I passed into the spirit world I did so without losing consciousness. I was able to gaze upon my physical body which I had just vacated, and a friend and colleague of my earthly days, who had passed on before me, came to me at the instant of my departure from earth, and took me to my new home in the spirit world. After a brief survey of my new abode, my friend recommended that I should take a rest in view of the fact that I had just quitted a final bed of sickness. I did so in my own house. I allowed myself to lapse into a most delightful state of slumber, feeling that I had not a care in the world. When I awoke I felt in a vigorous and perfect state of health such as I had never experienced before. I do not know precisely how long I lay sleeping, but I was told it was very brief; indeed, of much less duration than the illness that had caused my passing into the spirit world.

In considering the painfulness or otherwise of the illness that causes death, I think that the length of the illness and its painfulness could be linked together, for they both give a form of fatigue to the spirit body, though this fatigue must not be thought of in terms of earthly physical fatigue. The two are not really comparable. With us there is no heaviness of the limbs, no aching joints, no leaden weariness that makes the very movement of ourselves a misery to us; nor yet must it be thought that our fatigue is comparable with your earthly mental tiredness, where you have the inability to focus the mind upon anything except for the briefest possible time. Nor, again, do we lack interest in our affairs, or feel restless and ill at ease. The word fatigue is the best that I can find. There really is no word that adequately describes the condition.

With you, who are incarnate, physical energy will be expended during the course of your daily life until such time as it is necessary for you to rest. Rest is essential to you if you are to continue to function upon the material plane of the earth. When you retire to rest and to sleep, and while your spirit body is absent, your physical body is replenished with the energy that keeps you alive and active. Your body is, as it were, charged with force enough to carry you through your day and beyond it, if necessary. It constitutes a reservoir of force.

With us it is different. Force is continuously flowing through us from the source of all life. We are a channel for this inexhaustible energy which flows to us according to our needs of the moment. We have only to ask for a greater supply of force for some special purpose or for the accomplishment of some particular task upon which we are engaged, and it is immediately forthcoming. We have no need to recharge ourselves through the medium of sleep as do you. Our fatigue—for want of that better word—is more in the nature of a desire for a change from what we are doing, whether it be pleasure or work which is occupying our energies.

A desire for a change from what we are doing is a natural one common to both our worlds, yours and ours, but with us prolonged activities never lead to literal tiredness of the limbs or of the mind. We could pursue the course of our work far, far beyond the limits that are imposed upon you of earth without any loss of efficiency in our task. We could, and we do, work for a number of hours that would seem incredibly long to you, without the slightest ill-effect either to ourselves or to our work.

There seems to be an idea among certain schools of thought upon earth that in the spirit world we are employed upon the same work for all eternity. Possibly this strange notion is but a variation of the absurd idea of a spirit life of 'eternal rest', upon which I have already spoken to you. The spirit world is not static, neither are all its inhabitants forever occupied upon the same tasks, unremittingly and never changing. The work may never cease, but there are regular occasions when we cease to work. Among the glories of the life in the spirit world are the opportunities for as constant change as taste demands. We do not stagnate, or travel in a groove from which we cannot extricate ourselves. The desire for change of some sort comes upon us—and we change forthwith. That is our fatigue as near as it is possible to describe it to you.

The rest of the newly-arrived person is frequently advisable, or necessary, to allow of adjustment of the spirit body to its new conditions of life. It has been accustomed to being very securely fastened to the physical body where it can receive whatever unpleasantness the physical body may be submitted to during the course of its earthly term. An alert mind can quickly throw off these physical repercussions and adjust itself to the new life. Other types of mind will be slower and more leisurely. The long and painful illness will be one of the unpleasantnesses to which I have just referred, and although an alert mind can soon clear itself of recent experiences, still it may take a little time, and so a period of rest is undergone.

In no sense is the spirit body impaired by any earthly illness that caused its permanent transference to the spirit world. But earthly illness reacts upon the mind, which in turn be-dims whatever natural brightness the spirit body may possess. It is purely a matter of thought and has no reference at all to the personal brightness of spiritual progression. No ill-health or illness can take that away. A period of rest will therefore restore the spirit body to its proper and natural tone, both of colour and harmony with its life and surroundings.

With us rest is a very elastic term. One may take rest through so many varieties of ways. Indeed, it is perfectly commonplace to see someone busily at work here displaying all the industry in the world, to discover that in reality he is resting! So that anyone may be resting for all there is to show to the contrary.

How is a person affected whose death is sudden and perhaps violent as well, which would include the person who is precipitated into the spirit world without warning, or that knowing the end of earthly life is imminent yet undergoes a violent transition? How would such a person fare?

It calls to mind the phrase that was once such a favourite with certain types of mind: launched into eternity. What dreadful images this stupid phrase must have conjured up in the minds of so many people. The awful tragedy of 'death' which all men must face. The terrible uncertainty of what was to happen after they had 'departed this life'. The fearful prospect of being marched before the Great Dread Judge. Most of them having been told that they were 'miserable sinners', the best that could be hoped for would be 'mercy', provided that they 'believed on' something or *other* that was so obscure in its meaning that they could not make head or tail of it, but which nevertheless possessed some magic means of 'saving' them. Which was it to be— Heaven or Hell? Most probably the latter, from their obvious failure to reach the impossible standard set by their religious 'teachers'. Of what is there to be frightened in eternity? To us one of the greatest and most glorious truths is the very fact of this same eternity. But of that I will speak in due course. For the moment our question is waiting to be answered.

In speaking of people passing into the spirit world suddenly, you no doubt will recall where, for example, failure of the heart's action is the cause, and where accident or some deliberate action causes an instantaneous transition. In the latter instance you would be forcibly reminded of what takes place during the evil times of war upon the earth. Such transitions as these are not what could be considered in any way normal had other conditions prevailed. Normal transition, from the point of view of the spirit world, is that wherein the spirit body becomes gradually and easily detached from the earthly body in a slow and steady process of separation. The magnetic cord, in such cases, will become detached from the earthly body gently, it will fall away naturally, just as the leaf falls from the tree in the autumn. When the leaf is in full life and vigour it requires a strong action to dislodge it from the tree. And so it is with the spirit body. In the young the cohesion is firm, but it gradually lessens as age increases. When people on earth reach the autumn of their lives, like the leaf of the tree, the spirit body is less firmly attached to the physical body.

One reads of people reaching a great age upon earth, and then one day, in apparently good health, they are found to have 'died' in the chair in which they were sitting. They have, in fact, gone quietly to sleep in a normal healthy fashion, and the magnetic cord has separated itself also in a normal healthy fashion. That is an ideal transition. When, therefore, the earthly body suddenly collapses and the organs cease functioning, as in the case of some illnesses, there is not a great deal of shock transmitted to the spirit body.

A person so situated will be in a state of great

bewilderment which will be increased by lack of knowledge of the ways of the spirit world. Orthodox religious views will also add their considerable weight to the general confusion of mind. And even in cases where a good sound knowledge of spirit life is possessed there is bound to be some little momentary confusion in the mind. That is impossible to avoid. The mind may have been focussed exclusively upon material affairs, and it would require a second or two to apprehend what has happened—to collect the faculties, to use the earthly term. How easy our work in the spirit world would be if all transitions were in the latter category.

It is when we come to transitions where the physical body is literally disintegrated, blown into fragments in a second of time, that the greatest distress and discomfort are caused to the spirit body. The magnetic cord is snapped off or wrenched away, almost as though a limb of the physical body were torn from its socket. The spirit body finds itself suddenly dispossessed of its earthly tenement, but not before the physical shock of disintegration has been transmitted to the spirit body.

Not only is there extreme bewilderment, but the shock has something of a paralysing effect. The person so situated may be incapable of movement for the time being. In many instances sleep will intervene. He will remain in the place of his dissolution, but we come to his rescue, and carry him away to one of the rest homes specially provided for such cases. Here he will receive treatment from experts, and ultimately the patient will recover his full health beyond any shadow of doubt. The cure is certain and complete. There is no such thing as a relapse or a recurrence of the indisposition. Perhaps the most difficult part of the treatment comes when a full consciousness is restored, and the patient begins to ask questions!

What effect, you might ask, does maiming of the physical body have upon the spirit body? None whatever, as far as the full complement of limbs and organs is concerned. Disintegration may be sudden, or it may take a number of earthly years through the normal processes of decomposition. Whichever way it may take place, the result is the same—a complete, or almost complete, disappearance of that physical body. The physical body is corruptible, but the spirit body is incorruptible. And what applies to the whole in the latter also applies to the limbs and organs, in fact, to every part of the spirit body. The loss of one or more limbs of the earthly body, the possession of diseased organs, physical malformations, any subnormal or supernormal conditions of the physical body, any or all of these states leave the spirit body entirely unaffected. Whatever has happened to the physical body, the spirit body will always maintain its complete anatomy.

But the spirit body can assume very hideous *spiritual* malformations. These have nothing whatever to do with the formation of the physical body but are due solely to the kind of life that its owner has led upon earth. The malformations are various expressions of the hideousness that is resident within the mind, on many occasions that have found their outward expression in evil deeds of every description. These, however, do not come within the purview of our question.

People who believe that after their 'death' there will be a bodily 'resurrection' are often times puzzled in mind as to what will happen if they are not possessed of their full number of limbs, or, what is worse but more common, if their earthly body completely vanished in the course of time, or is instantaneously disintegrated. The trouble comes from the use of the word resurrection. Such people imagine that the normal procedure is for the physical body to rise up from its grave if it should possess one—at some future and unspecified date, whereupon it would find itself in the spirit world. It is fondly supposed that missing limbs would be restored and impaired faculties renewed, or if necessary, the physical body would be reintegrated after the fragments, in some inconceivable manner, have been collected and reassembled after their total disappearance.

The whole conception is, of course, fantastic. Once dissolution has taken place, the physical body is finished with as far as its former owner is concerned. It has no place whatever in the spirit world. It cannot enter there. And there is no magical process in existence that can so alter its constituents or form or mode of being as to be able to penetrate into spirit realms of any degree of height or lowness, of light or darkness, whatsoever. A profession of faith that such a thing is possible is of no avail; it simply cannot happen because it is against the laws of the spirit world. And these are natural laws, not laws that have been enacted by someone and can therefore be suspended or annulled at will.

To carry the matter still further, there is no such thing as resurrection of either the physical body *or of the spirit body*. As far as the spirit body is concerned, there is no 'rising'. There is simply a continuity of existence, From the moment that life is given to the physical body, the spirit body is also in existence. The earthly body comes to the end of its life; it ceases to function and so to provide an earthly vehicle for the spirit body, and the spirit body is released and *continues* its life in the spirit world, in its proper element and its true home. No resurrection has taken place. Nothing of the sort is needed. It has nothing to wait for, no Day of Judgment or other unpleasant prospect. The spirit body is free at last, unencumbered by its heavy earthly body; free to move and breathe, and enjoy the beauties of the realms of light.

And now, I think we have lingered long enough upon the threshold of the spirit world, and it is time that we passed through the great portal into the realms of light, where we can discuss other matters not so closely connected perhaps with the actual dissolution of the physical body.

Let us consider the spirit body and discuss some questions of its life in the spirit world, and perhaps in the process we may be able to smooth away a difficulty or two.

II

THE SPIRIT WORLD

I mentioned the word eternity to you just now. It is a word that implies so much but that in reality conveys so little to the average earthly mind.

The earth dweller would say, in effect, that eternity is like immortality—you cannot prove it. How can it possibly be proved that a certain state of existence, namely, that of the spirit world, will continue for ever, *without end*, to employ perhaps a more emphatic term. Just so. It is a difficulty that we all appreciate in the spirit world. And I would hasten to say that I am not going to attempt to prove it!

But I can do this. I can set before you one or two considerations that will serve to draw your mind towards the major differences between your incarnate state of existence upon earth and our discarnate state of existence in the spirit world. And in doing so there may emerge just a faint glimmering of what the word eternity can suggest.

If you will give the subject a brief moment's thought you will be forcibly reminded of the *impermanence* of life on earth. Living, as you do, with reality—for so you would term it manifested to you so very obviously in life itself and all that goes to constitute living upon earth, with, for example, the buildings that surround you, the ground upon which you walk, the food you eat, the clothing wherewith you cover yourself, your daily occupations and recreations, your comings and goings over short distances and long; confronted as you are with all these evidences of being—and many others besides yet you *know* that upon one day in your life the moment will come when you must leave all these 'realities' behind you to undergo the natural process of the dissolution of the physical body—in a word, when you will 'die'.

But before that event occurs, and during the whole of your life on earth, you will observe the process of disintegration going on all around you. Firstly, yourself. You will become older, the signs of which are sufficiently familiar to you to need no mention of them. Your clothes are constantly wearing out and need replacement. The furnishings within your home undergo the same process and require the same remedy. Your very house is in a constant state of decay, though not always visible to the eye, until one day repairs of one sort or another will be demanded. Call to mind, also, the many articles of daily use that by accident you can break—even your own bones are not immune from that! So that there is constantly going on around you this action of decay. Everything about you on earth is corruptible. There is, then, a palpable state of *impermanence*. However much the decay may be arrested, you still have the certain fact of the eventual termination of your earthly life, which in itself sets the seal upon mundane impermanence.

Now let us contrast all this with life in the spirit world and with the dwellers therein. Perhaps one of the most heartening, reassuring of feelings that we in the spirit world can harbour is the feeling of *permanence*. Firstly, as to ourselves. We are incorruptible. We have shed our earthly and corruptible bodies as we entered the spirit world, and we stand as we truly are, incorruptible. We do not age. On the contrary, *we grow younger* if we should happen to have passed our prime of life when we left the earth. That in itself is something in which to make one rejoice, but most of all, to make one feel secure and *permanent*. Our clothes do not wear out, or deteriorate in any way. Our homes are governed by the same law of incorruptibility. In my own home, for instance, I have never been obliged to make replacements or renovations in any single detail, whether of interior furnishings or structurally, since I first came to take up my residence here upon leaving the earth.

And it is the same with all other folk in these realms. I have made alterations, certainly; we all do that, but not because of decay or breakage, or wear and tear. What alterations we make are carried out for the pleasure they may bring to us and our friends.

The imposing buildings which are such an outstanding feature of these realms—among so many outstanding features—as clean and fresh and sparkling as upon the day when they were first erected. And when I tell you that no spot of decay or deterioration or dirt or dinginess can ever be detected upon any one of them, and when I also tell you that a great many of them have been standing there for *thousands of years,* I think you will agree with me that we are fully justified in considering ourselves and all that is about us and surrounding us in the agreeable light of *permanence.*

These few details I have given you are not one tithe of the numberless signs of permanence which are for ever presenting themselves before our minds. So that, if we cannot prove that our life here in the spirit world will continue for ever, we have abundant evidence for entertaining the strong probability that it *will* do so. And I assure you that nothing can give us cause for greater satisfaction than that. For us the words, 'for all eternity', would form a fitting clause in our charter of spiritual freedom.

I have often spoken of the magnificent buildings in the spirit world, but I have not so far made any reference to the particular form of architecture they favour. In fact, we have all types, from the earliest forms known to you on earth down to those of the present day. A type that is a great favourite among us here is that which is commonly known to you as Gothic. But all ages are represented. It would not be accurate to say they are reproduced, because here we can call upon people of a former age to erect buildings in the exact pattern of those of their own times. Beautiful though the various styles of architecture may be, and they are beautiful, yet to my mind the materials of which the buildings are composed, with their exquisite colourings, are still more lovely. Even the plainest structure, one that is perhaps almost devoid of external embellishment, is none the less a delight to see. All buildings, from the unpretentious cottage to any one of the stately halls of learning, look clean and fresh. But in addition, the materials of which they are constructed have a semi-translucence, an alabaster-like appearance with a superb variety of delicate colourings that seem to change their tones as the beholder changes his viewpoint. Some of them give the impression of being composed of mother-of-pearl in the most pleasing and restful shades of colours and tints. These colours are, of course, neither too vivid nor too brilliant where buildings are in fairly close proximity to one another. When more widely separated they can take on a more brilliant hue without disturbing the harmony of, or conflicting with, an immediate neighbour.

Whatever form of spirit world architecture you may care to consider, you must always remember the two extra factors of the materials of which they are made, and their wide range of gentle colourings.

There is one class of building that we do not favour, and that is the great gaunt barrack-like structure, rectangular or of any other shape, with rows upon rows of cheerless windows. Such buildings would not comport with the warmth and geniality of these realms, and would seem altogether too cold and forbidding, in spite of the lustre of our building materials and their diversified colours, to find any response from the dwellers here. And without the cordial response of the inhabitants of these realms nothing would remain in evidence very long. It is because we like what we have here that we have it, and that it survives.

If I were to say that we have in the spirit world that type of domicile known to you on earth as 'family mansions' it would no doubt conjure up in your mind the private ownership that is entailed in possessing a large mansion on earth.

Of course, there is ownership in the spirit world. Indeed, why should there not be? Ownership, however, is gained in a different way from that of the earth. There is only one right of ownership in the spirit world, and that is the spiritual right. None other will suffice; none other even exists. According to our spiritual right, gained by the kind of life we have lived upon earth, and afterwards according to our progression in the spirit world, so can we possess.

Many people arrive here to find themselves richly and abundantly provided with spirit-world possessions that are far in excess of those which they owned upon earth. And the contrary is often the case. Possessors of great earthly effects can find themselves spiritually poor when they come here. But they can gain the right to possess more, far more than they ever could own on earth, and of far greater value and beauty.

But to return to the large mansion-houses of which

I spoke. These are not erected through a wish to indulge a mere desire of possession, though naturally there is nothing discordant with the harmony and laws of these realms to take a delight in whatever we may possess, from the smallest trifle to the largest building. These mansions are usually built up from smaller houses by making structural additions from time to time. But the latter are made with a very distinct purpose, a purpose that has for its intent not the enlargement of the building for its own sake, but to carry out some useful, interesting, or helpful intention that will be of service to many others in these realms.

One particular house I have in mind first began its existence as a moderate-sized dwelling somewhat similar to my own home. The owner of it is an artist and musician, and when he first started his new life here, he had a great ambition to make his house a small centre for other artists and musicians, a meeting-place where kindred souls could forgather, the artists to discuss their art as it exists in the spirit world, and the musicians to perform such works as their fancy chose.

Gradually this little scheme took upon itself larger dimensions, far larger than were originally contemplated, until the house became much too small and insignificant for the worthy purpose to which it was being devoted. Additional rooms were built, and the whole house was extended in one direction and another. Finally, an apartment was added that resembled the 'great hall' customary in large mansion-houses on the earth. Since that time it has extended its hospitality to scores of friends, and there is never a period when the house is devoid of visitors. It is a beautiful residence to look upon; a delightful one to reside in, and we have often joined one or other of the numerous assemblages there when we have taken a holiday from our work.

Instances could be multiplied where such great mansions have their existence here, each of them devoted to some serviceable purpose for the entertainment of us all. They are not halls of instruction, the latter being of an entirely different nature both architecturally and in the purpose for which they are used.

The mansion-houses are the homes of individuals in precisely the sense that my house is my own home, but their great size is due solely to the design for which they were erected, namely, hospitality and entertainment, recreation and pleasure.

As to the ownership of the ground upon which these houses stand, the ownership, such as I have explained to you, resides with the occupier of the house. As the house is extended in size, so also is the area of the grounds which are attached to it. The larger the mansion, the larger the tract of ground which surrounds it. Anything in the nature of cramping would materially detract from the grandeur of the edifice.

All these mansions are set in the most beautiful park land where it is possible and permissible to wander to one's heart's content. There are no petty restrictions, no exerting of 'rights', no prohibiting notices, for there is nothing—and no one—to prohibit! The inhabitants of the mansions know that there will be no unwarrantable intrusion simply because we observe all the courtesies that it is common to expect among those who respect each other for their spiritual worth.

The woods and park lands are a dream of enchantment to wander in, and many are the occasions when we have strolled through them, or rested beneath the trees, while the deer, friendly and unafraid, have come to us and made themselves acquainted. They are beautiful creatures, enjoying such freedom as only the spirit world can give them, and they form an integral part of the superb landscape.

'Do we have churches in the spirit world?' is a question, I am persuaded, that will form itself in many minds, because what you call the 'afterlife' is associated, in some form or another, with religion. An 'afterlife' is a concomitant of religion, and while the state known vaguely as 'heaven' may be a tenuous reward for the 'good', there is always 'hell' with which to threaten the 'wicked'.

If an ecclesiastical edifice is an indispensable adjunct to religion upon earth, then the establishment of churches would benefit the peculiar state of the 'afterlife', whatever it may be. That is what many people think, and this attitude of mind finds outward expression in the spirit world. Yes, there are churches here, and very beautiful they are.

They are, of course, in keeping with all other buildings, being constructed of the same kind of materials, and having the same degree of care lavished upon them. Some people are considerably surprised to find such places here when they make their advent into spirit lands. I can number myself among them. Others, as I have hinted, more or less expected to find churches fully established in whatever 'heaven' to which their earthly religion had safely conducted them. The discovery helped to make them feel more 'at home' in their new surroundings, and they very soon become active members of the community attached to the church.

In these realms one will find churches of most of the denominations with which you are familiar. My own former religion is fully represented, and what is known as the Established Church also. But there are others besides, each with its own buildings. I have been into many of them. They all possess a calm, restful atmosphere in which it is very pleasant to spend a few thoughtful moments. When there is stained glass in the windows beautiful effects are created by the external light as it pours in from all quarters, while the rays meet and blend into colourful rainbow shafts.

Some of the churches are exact replicas of buildings that are in existence now upon earth. Others are what the earth would call restorations of once famous abbey churches, and so forth, that have fallen into ruins on earth. Here they have risen in all their architectural glory to grace the countryside with their presence.

The church buildings vary in size from what would be considered a small chapel to great cathedral churches, all of them erected and upheld by their devoted congregations.

How such things come to exist in the spirit world may cause you some wonder, since one would have thought there was no place for further religious differences and creedal distinctions. Most people do so think, but there remains a large residue who are still firmly wedded to their old earthly religious persuasion. Religious beliefs can take a very secure hold upon the minds of some persons. When they arrive in these realms they are fully convinced that their particular beliefs are alone responsible for their being where they are, which they regard as 'heaven', their just reward for their true faith. The fact that they led good lives in the service of others on earth they would sweep aside as of very little account in the great reckoning which has taken place. It is their faith, and their faith alone, they aver, which has brought them to these realms of heaven. They cannot be made to see that their great faith has availed them nothing; that they are where they are, not because of their faith, not in spite of it, but utterly regardless of it, and that it is their life of service to their neighbour, just that and that alone, which has brought its reward. The faith persists, sometimes elaborated with ritual and ceremonial, sometimes left plain and unadorned, simple and rather crude. And while it so persists their spiritual progression and evolution are at a standstill. They remain where they are in an environment of their creation.

The laws that allow of their religious practices are strict and must be obeyed. Adherents to each form of religion must confine their practices solely to themselves. There must be no endeavouring to convert others to their beliefs. Their outlook, as you can imagine, is foreshortened. They can and they do enjoy their 'heaven', home-made though it be, until one day spiritual enlightenment will come to them. Then they will emerge from their restricted, circumscribed life into the greater world that has been round about them all the time, had they but realised it. They will leave their useless creeds and dogmas behind them, and march forward upon the road of spiritual progression and evolution. They will then regard their churches as beautiful structures put to an entirely wrong use. They now see that as they regularly stepped out of their churches at the conclusion of a service, they stepped out into a world of truth, of truth which was not resident within the church's four walls.

Now a word as to the ministers who conduct the services in these. churches. They are men who were clergymen on earth. There is no lack of ministers for different churches. In fact, the supply is largely in excess of the actual demand. But that makes no real difference, since a number of ministers can work together in the same church, and so provide a fuller and more elaborate ceremonial in such establishments where it is performed.

After their earthly labours, their work here seems very light to them. Indeed, they have precious little to do beyond conducting their services. But then, you must remember that they consider themselves in 'heaven', and to take a few services and spend the remainder of the time in comparative idleness is simply the 'eternal rest' of which they spoke so glibly when they were upon earth. The members of their congregation are eternally resting, too. So that they are happy enough in their own limited way. They have arrived where they are through the kind of life they led when on earth, and here they have stayed while a sort of spiritual somnolence has descended upon them. They live that life of 'piety' which they thought so much about, and they are thankful for the church's help in getting them where they are.

The clergy are of all ranks in ecclesiastical orders, from learned prelates to simple parish clergymen. We have attended several of the services in these churches and listened to the sermons. It was an interesting experience.

Orthodox religion upon earth has much, very much to answer for. It forges many spiritual fetters which bind up the minds of countless souls upon earth, so that when they come here, we in the spirit world have to find means to strike off the irons that shackle them, so to release them to that freedom of spirit which is the natural, right, and proper mode of living in these lands.

When the earth becomes truly and completely enlightened in the knowledge of life in the spirit world, all these churches will be put to a different use. They will cease to be repositories of creeds and dogmas, and become true temples of the spirit world. And in the true temples of the spirit world something very different from what you call 'communal worship' takes place.

In the centre of the city in these realms there is a

great temple, a magnificent structure. It forms the very hub of the city from which everything radiates in every direction. It is a huge edifice, capable of seating thousands of us without any fear of crowding or other unpleasant conditions. It is encompassed by the most beautiful gardens, and as soon as one comes within the precincts one feels the most astonishing flow of power that emanates not only from the great wealth of flowers, but from the very building itself. This outpouring of force never diminishes.

Now, this is a temple of thanksgiving, not of worship as the earth understands it and professes to practise it. We do not congregate here to offer up so-called 'sacrifices'; nor do we perform elaborate ritual and ceremonial. Indeed, we do not perform either the one or the other at any time. We are not wearied by long and mostly unintelligible readings from ancient writers of a date so remote that they have no application to our present purposes and needs. We do not recite gloomy extracts from psalms which the majority of people do not understand. We do not sing hymns with whose sentiment we are either entirely out of tune or disbelieve in altogether. And lastly, we are not treated to the recitation of long, wordy, fulsome prayers that mostly breathe blatant flattery in their every sentence, and propound the most abstruse theological doctrines, as to the meaning of which one is utterly at fault. We perform none of these useless exercises. Instead, we meet here on special occasions, not by rule, not by habit, not because it is a duty, not because it is the 'right thing to do'; we meet here not because God 'demands' corporate worship as His right, not because some spurious authority proclaims that we must do so —or take the consequences.

We meet because on the special occasions to which I have just referred most illustrious beings from the higher realms come to visit us in this temple, beings who are close to the Great Source of all life and light. They bring with them some of the transcendental fragrance of those higher states of existence, and we are permitted to bask, as it were, in the radiance of the power and light they bring. Such power and light are partly of themselves and partly from their exalted realms, but chiefly from the Great Source of all.

The principal visitant on these occasions gathers together our heart-felt thanks for all that is given to us, for all that we possess, and he transmits them to the Giver.

Such a 'service' is simple and unpretentious, and above all things it is short. Most of these gatherings last not much longer than fifteen minutes or so of earthly time. But into that brief space of time is concentrated an act of inspiring beauty such as the longest, most elaborate, and most spectacular church ceremonial upon earth could never achieve in hours of pontifical pageantry with little or nothing underlying it.

We can please ourselves whether we shall be present or not, and we are not thought any the worse for being absent. Sometimes many of us are absent upon important work at the time of these visits, but we enjoy the benefit of them on another occasion, and in the meantime our thoughts go out to the visitants. But it is the same in this as in all things here. Once you have experienced some of the delights of these realms you never wish to forgo further such experiences, if it can possibly be helped.

We have other and smaller temples distributed throughout the realms, where there is carried on upon a smaller scale the same description of visitation that takes place in the great central temple. Some of the smaller temples are fashioned exactly like the churches with whose form you are familiar upon earth. This is an ideal realised—a church as you know it, devoted to its true purpose, and not merely a stage upon which is enacted a great deal of worthless ceremonial which has no spiritual significance and certainly no spiritual effect.

Upon earth an act of religious 'worship' implies in the minds of most folk an act of propitiation to a God who constantly demands it as His right. The Great Father of the Universe then ceases to be a Father and becomes an omnipotent being of uncertain temperament and most uncertain temper. Self-abasement, conciliation, worship, adoration, and a multiplicity of other emotions are what orthodox religions tell you must be your attitude towards the Great Creator. And to crown this gross and libellous conception of the Father of the Universe, you are told that you should—indeed, you *must*—love Him.

Orthodoxy, in one form or another, has claimed a monopoly of the 'life hereafter', and therefore all that appertains to it has been regarded in a strictly religious sense. The spirit world has thus become a world of piety, of sanctity, of righteousness—how the latter word is relished by some types of churchmen! Heaven, these same churchmen would say, is a holy place, a place sanctified by the presence of angels and saints, where a continuous stream of worship ascends to the Great Throne above. And so on earth you must have Divine Worship, and it is the *duty* of every citizen, according to his religious persuasion to attend once a week at some place of worship. A great many do so without the remotest notion of what they are doing or the lesson for doing it. They have only the crudest ideas concerning a Supreme Being, such ideas as they have, are derived from their religious teachers.

At last, when they pass into the spirit world, they bring all their crude notions with them. But as there are no laws here against thinking what you like, they continue so to think along the same old lines. Perhaps it would be more accurate to say that they do not think at all. But we who have our spiritual freedom know just what the term worship is worth.

We do not worship, as the earth understands the term. We pour out our eternal thanks for the happiness that is ours, a happiness that is itself magnified by the thought and the knowledge that still greater happiness lies ahead of us all. We are consumed with the deepest and truest affection for the Great Being who so lavishly bestows so many good things upon us.

After this slight digression, let us return to our discussion of architecture. Of all the types of buildings to be found in the spirit world, and those which will interest my friends on earth, the most numerous, by far, are the dwelling houses, the 'private' houses and cottages in which we live. They are of all kinds known to you on earth. But the appearance of our houses is very different from the appearance of earthly houses. The principal distinction is, of course, in the building materials, as I have indicated to you in the case of the churches here.

Although we have houses constructed of brick or of stone, as well as the half-timbered variety which is so popular here, your mind will inevitably be drawn to your own acquaintance with such buildings upon earth. But bear in mind what I have told you about the quality of the materials, with their particular and colourful external appearance, and you will see wherein lies the very great difference between your houses and ours. But there are other and important distinctions.

You must know, then, that we are never crowded for

space here. You will never see rows upon rows of dwellings, each contiguous with its neighbour upon both sides, each built upon precisely the same plan and design, and altogether presenting to the eye a dreary, unimposing, unimaginative line of depressing uniformity. In these realms each house stands completely detached in its own grounds or garden. There is adequate space in which to move freely around and about the house without the constant feeling of being hemmed in.

Of the gardens surrounding our houses I will speak to you in a moment or so.

In the spirit world we are not governed—or hampered—by certain conditions of the first importance which must be considered when building an earthly house. Firstly, upon the outside of our houses we have no unsightly pipes to carry off rain-water or the water that is used for domestic purposes; nor do we have gutterings upon the edges of the roof. We have no rain here—or snow. So that feature will be absent in our houses, and they look all the better for it, as you can imagine.

Now as regards the aspect of our houses. We have no need to think about which point of the compass our residence shall face. With you upon earth, it is the desire of most folk to obtain as much of the sun's light and warmth as possible, hence the desire that the home shall face towards the sun, with the principal rooms situated on the sunny side of the house. But here, the sun shines perpetually, a great central sun, and it shines with equal intensity from all directions. Its light penetrates with the same constant luminosity into every room in the house, irrespective of the room's position. The front of the house will be as bright during every moment of its existence—I cannot say during every moment of the day, because we have no day, and therefore the phrase in its earthly sense becomes meaningless from our point of view—the front of the house will always be as bright as the back.

And in speaking of the back of the house, here again I can show you a notable difference between our houses and yours. Strictly speaking, our houses have no backs to them as do yours. With you, the chief entrance is usually situated in the front, and architectural features are more pronounced in front than they are at the rear of the house. With our dwellings we make no such distinction, chiefly because the interior disposition of our homes omits certain features that are superfluous in the domestic life of the spirit world. As you know, we have no need for food and drink, so that we do not require the indispensable earthly kitchen. The space, therefore, that would upon earth be occupied by this culinary necessity, is devoted to other purposes in the spirit world homes. We have no lack of uses to which we can put such rooms.

I am giving you this description of our homes in a somewhat detailed form. Although many of you may be cognizant of the fact that we have houses in the spirit world, yet many important considerations are apt to be overlooked touching these houses of ours. Such details may seem trivial to some minds, unworthy of a moment's thought, yet, to others the import of what I am telling you, and of what I am going to tell you, will present itself in all its fullness.

These very details help to make up our life in the spirit world because they concern our homes, and our homes concern our lives, *just as they do with you.* And that is my very point. You who are upon earth do not know what it is to *live*, really to live. And you will never know until you come here for all time. So that it is only by comparing some of the 'trivial' details of our respective modes of living that you can gather any kind of idea of this perfect land in which I live. Merely to give a broad sketch of our life in the spirit world might be satisfactory as far as it goes, but it would leave a great deal unsaid. Much detail would be missing, and it would thus be left to your imagination and speculation to supply the missing information necessary to make a fuller and more comprehensive picture.

To wave aside such particulars as I am giving you because they seem trivial and very earthly and unworthy of consideration when 'heaven' is under discussion, is to hold a totally wrong conception of spirit lands. We are live people living in a beautiful land, a land far more solid than the earth. We love the countryside and the city; we love our houses and gardens; we are blessed with delightful friends. But the country and the city; the houses and the gardens; and, lastly, our friends have more substance about them than can be found upon earth, and this substance is made up of such details as I am describing to you.

It is of no use assuming a lofty attitude—as do so many people of earth—and say, in effect, that if 'heaven' is like that, why then, it is no better than the world in which we are living now. Or, at least, it is not much better, with its houses and churches, and rivers, and so forth. I would ask such people to be honest with themselves, to be truthful with themselves, and consider, if they do not like the things I am sketching to you, to formulate clearly and distinctly in their minds exactly what they *would* like. In other words, to specify, *exactly and in detail*, just what they want and just what they expect in their mode and form of life after they have 'died'.

At least I can give them this hint: from long

experience I can positively assert that these particular people of whom I am speaking would be thoroughly miserable in the 'heaven' fashioned from their ideas of what 'heaven' ought to be. Many such people have told me that they were profoundly thankful to find things as they are and not as they stupidly thought things ought to be.

Once again, I am afraid, I have digressed. But I have been urged that it is necessary to stress the fact that the spirit world is more real and its inhabitants more alive than the earth and its inhabitants can ever be. And, moreover, I must stress the fact that the world and the life I am trying to describe to you are not the impossible imaginings of pure Utopianism. The spirit world is a *real* world, peopled with *real* individuals.

Life upon earth is composed of many items, and they are familiar to you as part of everyday life. So it is with us here. Now think for yourself just how many such items will constitute one day in your earthly life. Begin with the moment of your rising in the morning, and continue until you return to your bed at night. You will be surprised at the sum total of details consisting of various actions and experiences. It is the same with us here, but with us all those harassing and troublous minutiæ of daily life are absent.

And now let us return to the house which I was describing for you.

As you have seen, by the omission of certain features necessary in your earthly houses, we are enabled to have greater space in our houses and to devote it to much pleasanter occupations and purposes.

It might be queried: what do you actually do with the extra rooms now that you have them? The answer is a simple one: we use them! They are not merely 'spare' rooms, useful when a visitor comes to stay with us, or convenient to use as a lumber-room. We have no lumber!

Let us examine the matter more closely. From whichever quarter of the house one may look, there is a magnificent view to be seen. Here, then upon the ground floor are the possibilities of a number of distinct and separate viewpoints from which to see the beautiful countryside. The number of rooms upon the ground floor is amply justified by the different views that are to be obtained from them, apart altogether from the variety in the planning and arrangement in the rooms themselves and the several uses to which they may be put.

Now let us mount the stairs and investigate the upper regions. The first thing we shall want to do is to gaze out of the window from our new and higher point of vantage at the same glorious countryside that surrounds us. Apartments which, on earth, would be bedrooms are, in the spirit world houses, used as sitting-rooms or living rooms, or utilised for whatever purpose takes your fancy—a study, perhaps, or for some form of recreation and amusement. Our friends will like to come and see us in these or in any other of our rooms, and we often find that our friends have a strong predilection for one or other of the apartments, which affords them pleasure in some way. And that alone is sufficient justification for our having *that* particular room. They may like our individual style of decoration in any or all of the rooms, and that, too, will add to their joy.

As far as the rooms themselves are concerned, they will vary just as much as do those in earthly houses, both in their size and their appointments. The beauty of the building materials is not confined merely to externals. Every fitting, every fixture (to use familiar terms), every thread of upholstery, the carpets on the floors, all are alike beautiful. The chairs in which we sit, in fact, the furniture in general, are in keeping.

You who have only seen earth world furniture can have no possible conception of the richness of spirit world furniture. We have no mass-production methods; each piece of furniture, from the simplest article to the most elaborate, is the work of a master craftsman whose pride in his work is only exceeded by our pride in the great dispensation that can provide such treasures for our greater joy and happiness. Much of the furniture which I have since added to my home contains some of the most exquisite carving it is possible to imagine; such carving, indeed, one could never have believed to exist. Even the simplest piece of furniture can be so treated as to make it fit for a king— to use the old expression.

There is absolute freedom of choice as to what type of house one shall inhabit. Once you have earned the right to own a house which is to be your home, you are at liberty to choose just the style of domicile that pleases you most. It may be one that you have longed for all your life upon earth, but thus far you have been unable to gratify your long-cherished desire. Here in the spirit world your wishes are at length fulfilled. Or you may wish to have your spirit home in the same style as your earthly home, if by chance the latter suited you and brought you contentment and satisfaction. That is what I did, not because my old earthly home was particularly beautiful. It was quaint—it still is—and it suited my temperament and desires, and I grew attached to it. When I came to the spirit world I found my new home to be the exact counterpart of my ancient earthly home, but with all the various alterations made to it which I had been unable to carry out upon earth, and which I had been desirous of doing, and no doubt would have done eventually had I not left the earth.

Houses, again, vary in size, from the small but picturesque cottage to the larger mansion-houses that I have already touched upon. One must not be misled by appearances in regard to the size of dwellings here. That is a rule I learnt very early in my life in the spirit world. Frequently, what on earth would be termed a 'humble' cottage, is here the home of a celebrity in some particular branch of human endeavour, a name that perhaps was a household word on earth. In the spirit world it is most unsafe to judge of the inmate by the size or shape or style of his dwelling. It is not that the owner of the cottage or small house is glad to live thus after living on earth in some rather palatial residence. It is rather that the charm of the cottage type of dwelling appeals to him, and no one will dispute his right to do as he pleases, and he will exercise that right still further when it comes to the matter of internal arrangements of whatever nature.

For example, we have no use for fire-places in our houses as a means of warming the room. We have no winter or autumn or spring in these realms. We have only the glories of perpetual summer. Winter-time on earth can have its beauties and grandeur in the countryside, with its leafless trees and dark earth, with the mist upon the landscape and the feeling of quietness while all nature seems to sleep. But winter can also have its miseries and unpleasantness. The bitter cold, the storms of wind and rain, the fog that descends and narrows the earth till distance is lost. Certain it is that you have the spring and summer to help to compensate for these trials, but who is there who would not wish to prolong the earthly summer far and beyond its allotted period, if it were possible? Now, if you were to take the most perfect summer's day upon

earth that you can recall to your mind, in so far as the
weather itself were concerned, you would still be far,
far below the splendour of the heavenly summer of
these realms. And with us every day is summertime.

Incidentally, we never become tired of it. I have not
found one single, solitary individual in these regions
who has at any time expressed the wish for a change of
weather. When you come here and sample it for
yourself, you will feel the same about it, I am certain.
If not, then you will be the one interesting exception
that will prove the rule!

You can see how this will affect not only our lives but
our homes as well. Our windows and doors can always
remain wide open; there is a genial warmth penetrating
into every nook and comer of our houses, just as the
light diffuses its rays throughout. There is therefore no
need to consider what means of heating we shall
employ when ordering the disposition of our home. But
a fire-place can itself be ornamental and pleasing to the
eye, and for this reason you will find them in many a
house. But other people prefer to dispense with them
altogether. Their absence in no way spoils the general
appearance of the apartment.

In their early days in the spirit world people will
often have fire-places in their homes, but as time goes
on and they realise the permanence of the glorious
summer, they abolish them. It is purely a matter of
choice, and we can all suit ourselves in the matter. But
whatever we do, we shall not be considered eccentric if
we wish to indulge some fancy. Our friends will recall
their early days in the spirit world when they were
similarly situated, and, accordingly, we shall have their
sympathetic support and co-operation in the fulfilment
of our desires, whatever they may be.

And now an important matter arises. How do we

arrange for the maintenance of our houses? By which I mean: who does the cleaning for us, and generally looks after things?—that is, those of us who need such help.

This is another point which irritates some minds. The incarnate person, upon the mention of spirit world houses, immediately thinks of them in terms of cleaning and upkeep, and the idea of houses in the spirit world then becomes distasteful.

Here again arises a confusion between your world and ours. Recollect what I have said about our world being incorruptible, and you will see at once that the two words *dust* and *dirt*, which are such a nightmare to those of my friends on earth who have the care of their own homes in their hands, simply cannot have any meaning in the spirit world. Dust and dirt are merely disintegration in progress, and so, where you have no disintegration, as in the spirit world, so you will have no dust and dirt.

Every house, here in these realms, is of a cleanliness where immaculate is the only term with which to describe it. Without the means to cause the dirt, you cannot have the dirt. With you on earth the gradual but persistent process of decay will always show itself in dust and dirt. You cannot avoid it. The most you can do is to invent and provide mechanical means with which to clear it away. But it will return and continue to return. I am, I know, stating what is a painfully obvious fact to so many good people, but I must do so to emphasise one of the outstanding qualities of our homes in this spirit world, namely, their superlative and everlasting cleanliness. In this respect, therefore, our homes will require no attention throughout the whole period of their existence, and that may be hundreds of years of your time. A house wholly unoccupied for such a protracted period would be, at the end of that time, as immaculate as on the first day of its erection. And that entirely without the least attention having been paid to it.

The fabric of the house comes under the same conditions, and these conditions are a law. We have no winds in the spirit world that will wear away the stones or bricks of which a house is built, nor do we have a smoke-laden atmosphere which will eat into the surface of our buildings or cause them to crumble away into dust. We have no rains to cause rot and rust to set in, and so to require various replacements. All our possessions within doors, our furniture and our hangings, our personal belongings, such as our books, all alike are subject to the same splendid law. They cannot deteriorate, receive damage, become soiled; the colours in our hangings and upholsteries cannot fade or become shabby. Things cannot get broken or cracked with age. We cannot lose our small possessions by mislaying them. The floor-coverings on which we walk can never become worn out with constant tread of feet.

And there are people who will say: 'Why, the spirit world has houses with furniture, and so on. It is scarcely better than life on earth!' Scarcely better than life on earth, indeed! Very well. Such people are at liberty to spend their spirit life in a field, if they so wish, but for me, and for millions like me, I find immense contentment and pleasure in owning a house to be occupied under perfect conditions, some of which I have recounted to you.

We have spent some little time considering the house itself. Let us now wander out and inspect the gardens or grounds round about our homes. But before doing so I would like to revert to a subject which is not unconnected with the gardens themselves.

I have already remarked that we are never hungry,

from which it might be inferred that our social gatherings are entirely without refreshment. Such is not the case. We have the most delicious fruit in abundance. Our host or hostess, whoever it may be, will always see to that. But it is fruit that is very unlike yours on earth, we eat it for a very different reason, and it produces a totally different effect upon us. To take the fruit itself first. We have a much greater variety than do you, even taking into account the diversity to be found in the different parts of the world. All the fruits that you have we also have here, but with the quality there is no comparison. And the size, too, is remarkable. That you must see to believe!

The fruit contains a great quantity of nectar-like juice, at the same time leaving the flesh of the fruit firm to the hold. It is perfectly formed, without blemish, a picture to behold, and its appearance does not belie it, for it tastes even more lovely than it looks. In eating the fruit, we are not conscious of an internal satisfaction such as are you on earth with your fruit. We feel at once a powerful force running through our whole system, a feeling of exhilaration both mental and physical. We have no physical hunger that calls for satisfaction; whatever fruit we eat acts as a life force, and, as it were, stirs us up mentally and charges us with vigour.

It is difficult for you on earth to imagine yourself without hunger and the need for food. To be hungry and thirsty is instinct with human nature on earth. When you come to reside permanently in these realms of the spirit world, you leave your hunger and thirst for ever behind you. You will never, therefore, miss the food and drink for which you no longer have any need. And that state in turn becomes instinct with human nature in the spirit world. You would even find that you could manage very nicely if you were never to partake of any fruit here, but once you have tried it and sampled its rich benefits, you have discovered a pleasure that you will never want to deny yourself. And there is no need to deny yourself upon any grounds whatsoever. There is plenty of it to be had simply for the gathering of it, and you may 'tuck in' without fear of being dubbed a glutton!

Where does the fruit grow? Most people have a garden attached to their houses, and they are bound to have a favourite fruit tree tucked away in some corner that will amply supply them both for the requirements of hospitality and for their own personal needs. But there are large tracts of land here that are entirely applied to the growing of fruit of various sorts and for various purposes.

One of my earliest experiences after I had arrived in the spirit world was the discovery of a splendid orchard of fruit trees. The owner of it was quick to perceive that the illness that had caused my transition to these realms had been a short one, and he presented me with some fruit of a particular kind which, he said, would supply me with just that reinvigoration that I needed. Edwin was with me at the time (indeed, it was he who disclosed this orchard to me in the first instance), and although he had been many years here, he also partook of some fruit, greatly to his benefit likewise.

The whole of this orchard is a plantation of special fruit trees for the use of people who are newcomers to the spirit world. The owner of these trees—though I think he would prefer the appellation of 'custodian'—is highly skilled in selecting just the right kind of fruit for new-comers. Once you have called upon him, he expects you to call again as often as you please. If he should be away from home at the moment of your visit, he explains, you are to walk in and help yourself, and the fruit trees will themselves act the part of host—and a much better one, he would say, than himself—and do what is necessary. The fruit is always there because it is always in season, and it is always in capital condition for consumption.

The genial soul who conducts this fruit farm, if one can so term it, is performing a very great service to all of us here, and you can readily imagine that he possesses a great knowledge of the technicalities of his work. He is, in fact, an institution in these realms, and is known far and wide not only for the services he performs but for himself, for one could not find a more amiable companion. He is the owner of the orchard and the dwelling house that is close by. He, himself, will tell you that he holds the orchard in trust for the whole of this realm, and by virtue of his services thereto, he enjoys the privilege and pleasure of 'owning' it until such time as he will pass on to a higher state. And there is no one in these realms who would dispute not only his fitness for the services he renders, but his right to call the land, the orchard, and his dwelling house strictly his own for just so long as he wishes to extend his tenure of them. We shall be very sorry for ourselves when he transfers his noble activities to a higher realm, while we shall be happy on his account that he has reaped a rich and well-earned reward.

I have spoken to you of food in the limited extent of fruit, but what of drink? Do we never feel the need for liquid of some sort? Never. But you must know that there is an enormous quantity of juice to be found in the fruit which would be sufficient to quench any thirst of reasonable dimensions!

However, the spirit world is not an arid waste, as you will by this time have gathered. There is water in abundance in the rivers and streams and brooks, and every drop of it not only fit to drink, but, indeed, like no water to be found upon earth. It glistens and sparkles; it is crystal clear; it is buoyant; one can slip beneath its surface and enjoy its warm embrace as it folds its living arms about you. It soothes, it invigorates, it inspires. It will produce the most beautiful sounds when it is disturbed on its surface. The ripples of the wavelets will reflect back a multitude of rainbow tints and will emit the purest of musical tones. Have you any water like that upon earth? I cannot remember ever seeing any such when I was there.

There is no such thing as stagnant water here; every drop of it is everlastingly living water of jewel-like purity. We can bathe within it, we can ride upon its surface in many a splendid vessel, or we can descend beneath it without harm to ourselves, because it is our nature that no harm can come to us.

And now, after this slight digression, let us return to our consideration of the gardens.

Our gardens are as much like the earth gardens as our spirit world houses are like yours. The first difference that you will notice is the absence of fences, or hedges, or walls, or any other means of indicating the boundaries of our 'property'. So that, when you look out of the windows of your home in these realms, the whole wonderful prospect will seem like a gigantic park, beautifully wooded, with streams and rivers to be seen sparkling in the light of the central sun, and flashing back countless rays like veritable diamonds. Apart altogether from their beauty, our gardens have an eternal freshness and orderliness about them that would be impossible of attainment in any earthly garden. My use of the word orderliness must not be misconstrued into anything approaching the somewhat rigid regularity to be observed in the public gardens of the earth. Beautiful as the latter may be, there is something of a cold orderliness about them; a lack of the sense of friendliness; a severe ordering of the flowers in their precise arrangement. They seem to be so very much on view, and one may have the feeling of being warned off. Even the simplest of our spirit gardens is immensely superior to the most assiduously preserved garden to be found upon earth.

The differences between our gardens and yours are numerous, so numerous and wide, in fact, that the only real point of resemblance is in the name. I am inclined to think, though this is only my personal opinion, that the absence of fences and hedges to which I have just alluded; indeed, the absence of all marks of our own 'territorial frontiers', is one of the chief contributing factors to the great divergence between our gardens and yours.

In spirit world gardens one feels at once the sense and the reality of spaciousness which abounds everywhere. It is another instance of the freedom which we all know, feel, and enjoy. Freedom, you see, manifests itself in so many ways here, even in what might be deemed the comparatively unimportant matter of our gardens. It may seem unimportant to you who are still on earth, but to us here it is vital.

All our gardens, then, merge the one into the other, forming an unrestricted whole which constitutes the great countryside of these realms. The land is not entirely fiat, of course. There are gentle hills and slopes, delightful valleys with streams and rivers running through them. There are pathways winding their pleasant course beneath verdant trees of every kind. And every inch of ground is under cultivation of one sort or another. There is no barren land here, no neglected land. We each of us keep our gardens alive, in every sense of the term, by the affection which we shower upon them. There is no constant battle with weeds and wild growths; nor are we at the mercy of the elements, whether of wind or rain—or lack of rain; of cold or frost; or of too great heat.

In the perfectly tempered warmth of these realms every form of spirit nature has its full chance to grow, to flourish to its fullest extent, unhampered by such conditions as your earthly nature has to endure. If that is the case, it may be remarked, then there is no wonder that spirit world gardens are a perfect picture of heavenly delight. That is so, but it is a point that is so frequently overlooked, because people are apt to think too much in terms of the earth when considering life in the spirit world.

There is another feature marking the difference between our gardens and yours, and which will be of some interest to those of my friends on earth who are fond of gardening. With you in the earth world, once given the requisite ground, it will not be long before you will produce some sort of result by virtue of your possessing some general, though perhaps limited, knowledge of horticultural practice, and for the rest trusting to the plants to look after themselves, with occasional assistance from a more knowing friend. But a garden of the spirit world demands expert knowledge in its creation, not to prevent us from going wrong, but to produce any results at all. Without our knowing exactly how to produce flowers or other growing things, we should fail to create any garden whatever.

Most of us here have consulted the expert gardeners at one time and another, either in the first formation of our gardens or afterwards to make alterations and improvements. If we should lack ideas in the matter, these important functionaries will soon provide us with something of their own fashioning that will be sure to please us far more than we ever anticipated.

From time to time I have consulted with these good folk upon my own gardening arrangements, and it is astonishing how they have the faculty of knowing just what we most desire without our having expressed it openly. In any case, a hint is all that they require to evolve a dream of a garden, from the tiniest rustic nook to the great swelling banks of flowers with their innumerable colour schemes which are to be found in the neighbourhood of all the 'public' buildings in these realms. But more recently a sprightly young lad, named Roger, has taken up his residence with us, who is himself an expert horticulturist.

Shortly after his arrival here, and at whose transition Ruth and I assisted, he became greatly attracted to horticultural work, and he has since become highly proficient in the art. So that now the gardens of our small domain are under his constant supervision and we have no need to venture farther afield than our own home in all matters appertaining to their arrangement or re-arrangement with such an expert living on the premises. Roger here carries out all manner of experiments in floral disposition and display which is as great an interest to the rest of us as to himself. We are never quite sure what new form our 'grounds' are likely to take at any given moment, and our numerous friends are oftentimes treated, as we are ourselves, to many and varied horticultural surprises!

A great many of these expert horticulturists were either gardeners or lovers of gardens when they were upon earth. Being at liberty—as we all are here—to choose their occupation when they came here to live, it is but natural that they should put their previously gained knowledge to some further use, or that they should become fully occupied in what was on earth a diversion to be indulged in when time and opportunity permitted. It is true that a great deal of their earthly knowledge would be of little use to them as gardeners in the spirit world in any practical application, but it does not take them long to discard their old knowledge for the new, to exchange the earthly methods for the spirit world methods.

Not all of our gardening experts are practical gardeners. Some of them are designers of gardens only, leaving the actual creation of the garden to others. And others are creators of gardens only, leaving the designing to others. And again, some combine the two, designing and creating.

The horticultural architects are never at a loss for an idea, and you must know that designing a garden does not only mean arranging for the disposition of some small plot of ground such as one finds adjoining so many of the dwellings on earth. In the spirit world a whole countryside can be altered and rearranged down to the smallest detail, and the plans have to be made from which the actual creators are to work.

In the spirit world, planning and building a garden involves certain considerations which would not be heeded on earth. For example, the types of flowers and trees, with especial attention to their colouring, will largely be ordered or influenced by the kind of dwelling or other edifice which stands or is to stand in the particular ground. You will recall how the stones and so on in these realms are all glowing with beautiful shades of colour. The flowers in the gardens, therefore, will all accord with the colours of the masonry of the nearest building, broadly speaking, so that the two shall form together a blend of perfect harmony. Colour, you see, produces sound, and sound produces colour, so that it is essential that consonance and not dissonance should be the resulting effect of all horticultural efforts in these realms. Discord of an unpleasant nature would not be permitted. So here is one point, at least, where our gardening methods differ from yours.

Again, we are not restricted, as you are, to seasons of a year. Our flowers and shrubs and trees are always in bloom and in leaf. We have combinations of flowers in our gardens that would normally be impossible upon earth through the passage of time, or because of the order of nature upon earth that causes flowers to come to maturity, flourish for a brief period, and then fade and die.

You, who love the flowers and the gardens that grow them, can you not imagine our joy, here in these realms, where we have our favourite flowers always with us in our gardens, never at the mercy of the elements or the seasons, never withering with age, but ever presenting themselves to the world in all their beauty, in all their simplicity or their grandeur, in all their wide range of colourings, from the most delicate tint to the most vigorous and compelling of bright colours, and, lastly, always shedding their delicate perfumes upon the sweet pure air to delight us not only in the exquisiteness of their aroma, but to charge us with spiritual force—can you not imagine our joy at all this?

This is all very well, I can hear you say; but do you never become tired of all this perfection? With all this absolute perfection about you, how can you have any contrast, any light and shade? You surely need something that is not so perfect if one may so express it—to show off, to emphasize, what is perfect.

Certainly that is a point which might worry some people. The latter are dreadfully afraid that there may be a flaw somewhere in these details of spirit life which

I am giving you; some important matter, some
qualification which I have overlooked, that would tend
to show that these realms are really, after all, not quite
so perfect as one would be led to imagine. Or, in other
words, there is bound to be something, somewhere, that
we should dislike, or upon which we might frown in
displeasure.

Well, now, the details I am giving you are drawn
from my own experiences, first-hand experiences. I give
you facts as I and millions of others see them in these
realms; facts which we *know* to be the truth. There is
no disputing the colours of the flowers, for example, just
as there is no disputing thousands of other facts patent
for all to see and observe and realise their truth.

Or, again, you feel, shall we say, that what I am
telling you seems too good to be true. Perfection, you
would rightly say, is unattainable on earth, but that is
not to say that perfection does not exist somewhere else.
Perfection, it will be objected, admits of no qualification.
Either a thing is perfect, or it is not perfect. There can
be no half measures about it. One thing cannot be more
perfect or less perfect than another. That is the truth
in its strictest sense. But perfection can be largely a
matter of personal experience. We may imagine that a
thing is perfect because we have never experienced or
encountered anything better. We are therefore entitled
to regard this particular thing as perfect, and we shall
do no harm to ourselves or to any other person by so
thinking.

These realms wherein I live, are, to all of us who
inhabit them, a state of perfection so far as our present
experience takes us. The great majority of us can
scarcely contemplate a state of greater beauty and
happiness, that is, a state of greater perfection than
this sphere where we have our homes and our life. We

love every inch of these realms, we love every moment of our lives; we are supremely happy—we could not be more so; that is to say, we do not *think* we could be more so. But when we come to regard the strict truth we know that when we pass into a higher realm we shall be happier still. We have not yet enjoyed that experience, but those of our friends who have already mounted to a more exalted realm are continually returning to visit us and to tell us of the greater happiness which they are now enjoying, happiness which they did not think possible, and to speak of the *greater perfection* in their new realms of things which already seemed perfect to them. So that, perfection, after all, is a matter of degree, of comparison, of experience, and it is not possible to set any limitation upon perfection, because we do not know as yet how far it is possible for perfection to extend. So that when I say that everything here in these realms is perfect, I mean, of course, everything is perfect in so far as our present experience takes us.

And that applies to us all here. Even when we have visited higher realms for a period, however long or short, we have only *glimpsed* the *greater* perfection of those realms. We can see that things are immensely purer in all ways, the colours, the musical sounds, the flowers and forests and woods; the rivers and streams; and, lastly, the people themselves, all are more rarefied. But those of us who have been so fortunate as to have visited a higher state never on any account feel dissatisfied with our own estate upon returning to our own realms. Dissatisfaction does not come by visual comparison of our present realms with higher realms. There are other causes for that which, for the time being, we will not consider. As far as my description of these realms is concerned, you need not be afraid that it is all too good to be true. To you who are still incarnate it may seem that it is impossible of attainment. To us, it is our everyday life.

Why should I depreciate the true condition of things here? Why should I pretend that the conditions are less wonderful and less beautiful than they are simply because some folk, still living on earth, cannot imagine anything being better than the state of existence upon earth? What is there against the particular beauty and grandeur of these realms to which such exception is taken? Because the same people have not experienced either or both, it does not follow that they do not exist in these realms. And if, by a deliberate perversion of the truth, I were to describe this state as being but a fourth-rate imitation of the earth, people would still be displeased. What! they would say in effect—is the next world no better than this world?

There are many parts in the spirit world that are a thousand times worse than anything that can be found in the earth world. There are many regions in the spirit world that are immeasurably more beautiful and more glorious than could ever be found upon earth. Yet there are minds who are thoroughly dissatisfied to learn of either! They need not perturb themselves unduly. When they pass into the spirit world they will go to that place for which, by their earthly lives, they have fitted themselves, and to no other. And in addition, they will go only to that place, or that description of place, which they think 'heaven' ought to be. How long they will remain in their home-made 'heaven' rests with themselves, but my observations tell me that it is usually not very long before such people emerge from their restricted 'paradise' and join their fellows in the real 'heaven' that has been waiting for them all the while. It so happens that their ideas of what perfection is, or ought to be, do not coincide with what perfection really is, even in the qualified sense we have just discussed. In the end they are bound to admit their error of judgment!

It is strange—is it not?—this strong disinclination upon the part of some minds to accept the fact that some sections of the spirit world, at least, should bear any resemblance to the earth, albeit a resemblance that involves considerable modifications. After spending their lives in an earth world where such objects as houses and buildings of every kind are to be found, where the countryside with its fields and meadows, its rivers and lakes, its trees and flowers are but commonplace facts of earthly existence, some people feel resentful that they should be asked to live on in a future state where so many of the familiar landmarks of the earth are again in evidence.

Of course, they are not asked, strictly speaking, to live amid these surroundings, but we have already considered that point. It is more the fact that a spirit world civilization exists at all that so annoys some of our friends on earth. Again I would ask, what would they have in place of these natural surroundings?

The aversion, I am persuaded, arises from the notion that these realms of which I am speaking bear some limited or modified resemblance to the earth. Now that in itself is wrong. It is to imply that certain regions of the spirit world have been constructed upon earthly lines; that the earth has been taken as a model and the spirit realms built upon that model, and that they therefore constitute something of a replica of the earth. Exactly the opposite is the truth. The earth bears a limited or modified resemblance to these realms, which is a different matter altogether. Spirit lands, in the realms of light, are a thousand times more beautiful than any part of the earth it is possible to mention.

It will doubtless be pointed out to me that in spirit

lands there are houses that are a counterpart of earthly houses, and my own dwelling will be adduced as an example. That is true.

My own house came into existence in the spirit world after I had earned the right to have it there as my home, to be set apart for me until I should arrive in spirit lands to live. But domiciles in incalculable numbers, having no counterpart on earth, had been in existence hundreds and hundreds of years before ever I was born upon earth. The inspiration that came to man to cover himself and his family with a roof of however rude a description came from the spirit world. You may say: nothing of the sort; it is no more than a natural instinct exerting itself, an instinct of self-preservation, to protect one's self from the rigours of wind and storm, of cold and heat. If you feel that you must adhere to your contention, then, so be it. I cannot provide proof of my assertion yet. You must wait until you come to spirit lands yourself, and I shall be pleased to show you where you can ascertain the truth for yourself. In the meantime, I will adhere to my contention, and I will venture further to assert that the whole range of earthly architectural design throughout the ages has been inspired and influenced, promoted and encouraged by great minds resident in the spirit world.

Inspiration is not a matter of physical brain cells self-functioning in such a manner as to produce a clever or brilliant idea in the mind of a person. Inspiration can come from any quarter of the spirit world, from the highest realms, from the lowest realms, and from the grey lands as well. It remains with the incarnate as to which quarter of the spirit world he will lend an ear. If to the highest, there will come only that which is good; if to the lowest, only that which is evil and bad. In the former, among many other good things, you will have all the beauties of art and music, but they will be beauties and not hideous distortions masquerading under the cloak of pure art; you will have scientific discoveries for the benefit of mankind, as well as schemes for his well-being. You will have great works of dramatic and literary genius that will live through the years and never show signs of wear. From the dark realms you will have wars and strife, unrest and discontent; you will have literature that is a disgrace to so-called civilization, and music, even, that is an abomination of impure sounds, such sounds as would never exist for an instant of time in these realms.

No, the spirit world is not a copy of the earth. The spirit world was in being aeons of time before the earth came into existence. Does man think that he has formed and fashioned all that is man-made upon earth entirely of his own mind and genius, then man is woefully mistaken.

Without the spirit world, the earth and mankind, who is barely living as judged by the greater life of the spirit world, would soon get into inconceivable difficulties. The beauties of the earth are but a foretaste of the beauties of the spirit world and the life that lies before all mankind. We do not copy you who are on earth—we have no need to do so. We give you glimpses of the spirit world so that you may have some slight acquaintance with the spirit world before you come to take up your life and residence here.

We seem to have marched a long step from our discussion of spirit world houses and their gardens, do we not? But these other matters that we have looked into are all relative to our one subject, which is the consideration of the spirit world and the life we lead here.

And now, how are the residents of the houses composed? Are they family groups or single occupants?

Doubtless, you will call to mind such concentrations as you have on earth, but you must also remember that even on earth family groups are continually altering their composition. The children in an earthly family grow up, and for various reasons they leave their parental homestead—upon marriage, for example, or for reasons connected with their business or occupation. People on earth live alone for equally varied reasons. And so the changing of family groups is constantly going on. In normal times on earth, families live their lives with these changes taking place in their family ties, and eventually they come into the spirit world.

Upon earth the number of generations of a family is fairly limited, but in the spirit world all previous generations of a family are co-existing. So that it might reasonably be asked: who will live with whom? That, as you can see, will raise a very considerable problem if viewed from the strictly limited viewpoint of the earth. But it presents no problem to the organization of the spirit world. Family ties, *as such,* have little significance in the spirit world. Here the one deciding factor in this matter of human relationships and family ties, is the bond of affection and mutual interest that prevails between any two or more people. The rule applies in all circumstances. It applies to husband and wife, to brother and sister, to father and mother, and to all the remaining degrees of family relationship. And it applies to ordinary friendships between individuals of different families and between both sexes.

In the spirit world we are at liberty to live as we wish. If we desire to join forces with one or more companions, we shall soon be able to find others, similarly inclined, to unite with us and share the one domicile. Many of us here do that. Apart from mutual regard and respect and interest, we may all be occupied in the same type of work, and so, sharing our knowledge and experience, we live our lives together under the one roof, and in complete accord. If at any time we should wish to occupy a separate establishment we can do so without fear of hurting the feelings of our companions.

When I first came to the spirit world I found myself the possessor of a replica of my old home on earth. There it stood, fully equipped and ready for my instant habitation. Edwin, my old friend and colleague, undertook to show me a little of the new world I had just entered, and during our tour of inspection I met a very charming young person whose name is Ruth. She joined our small expedition, since there were many things that she, too, had not yet seen, and finally, after spending so much time together in our peregrinations, the three of us felt that we should like to work together if that were possible. It was possible, and we have so worked ever since. Ruth and Edwin are each the possessors of very charming houses, of which they are 'sole occupants', but we are so much together, the three of us, that Edwin and Ruth spend far more time in my house than they do in their own. Their homes are filled with their possessions and the things they value, but the prolonged absence of the owners makes no difference. They will always find their houses to be in the same state of good order whenever they wish to retire to them, as they do occasionally.

The same situation also applies to an old friend who has also taken up his residence with us. Gordon by name, he has but recently arrived in these lands. He had been in active communion and communication with us for a great many years of his earth life, and he was himself a powerful psychic instrument. It was a great pleasure to Ruth and me to assist at his passing, and to bring him to our home. He awoke to his new life to find himself reclining comfortably upon the couch in our

main room, through the windows of which he had the
first glimpse, as a permanent resident, of the land of
his new life. Ourselves apart, there were other friends
to welcome and greet him, friends of his earthly days:
two small sparrows, his dog, and two handsome pumas.
So that altogether our household is an animated and
lively one. We are living a happy life working together,
taking our amusements together, receiving our friends
together, and visiting together.

It is no uncommon sight to see such arrangements;
indeed, I think they preponderate in these realms. The
bonds that unite us are firm and undeniable, otherwise
the joint establishment would soon collapse. The plan
fits in with our particular temperaments and tastes and
desires, whether the latter be of work or of play. It is
the wish of all five of us that our present system and
arrangement of living shall always continue. And it will
so continue, until the time comes for one or all of us to
proceed to another realm in the natural course of our
spiritual progression.

There are many couples to be found living in
charming houses here; for example, a husband and wife
who were happily married when upon the earth,
admirably suited to each other, and with a real bond of
affection between them. Or there may be other family
groupings such as I outlined to you a moment ago. If
you remember that all these small communities are
formed not because of blood-relationship, but because
of mutual esteem and affection, you will always find the
answer to the question: who will live with whom—in
the residential relationships of the spirit world.

Other reasons apart, if spiritual progression brings
about the departure of some member of a household in
the spirit world, it might be thought that it would cause
some measure of unhappiness or sadness to the

remainder of the household. In such a case we should greatly miss the customary presence of our former companion upon his proceeding to a higher realm, but we should not feel the same rather blank despair as do you upon earth in other circumstances of departure. We have a keen appreciation of the greater happiness which will be the good fortune of our departed friend, and that will spur us on to attain our own progression, and so join him who has preceded us. But it is not by any means certain that we shall take our next step in progression when it comes, if I may so express it.

There are many people to be found in these and other realms, both higher and lower, who have earned for themselves their undoubted removal into a higher sphere of spiritual life, but who prefer to remain where they are for a variety of sufficiently good reasons. For example, some of the great teachers in these realms are fully entitled to live in a higher realm, and actually possess houses in those higher states, but they have chosen to remain where they are and carry on their present form of work. This act of self-denial is itself a means of still further progression, though it is to be doubted if any such thought ever enters the head of the individual who elects to adopt this course of action.

When I say teachers, I do not mean only teachers of spiritual truths and so forth, but instructors of all kinds in the various arts and crafts of these particular realms. There are thousands of people here who are learning some form of work that is new to them, details of which I have already recounted to you. In this case it is the work itself and the joy it brings in the service to their fellow-beings that prompts such folk to postpone their advancement of spiritual estate. One day, however, the time will come when they will be obliged to betake themselves into their rightful sphere since to remain longer in a lower realm might cause them some discomfort. But they can return whenever they wish and make prolonged visits to their old friends, and even resume for a limited period their former tutorial occupation, needless to say, to the extreme delight of their colleagues and pupils.

It is not only teachers who postpone their permanent elevation and remain where they are, although entitled to reside in a higher realm. It is open to anyone, without exception, to do the same whenever the circumstances arise. The circumstances, in fact, are many in which this can happen. To instance one case: two people are mutually attracted while upon earth, a husband and wife, shall we say. The wife passes into the spirit world and attains to a certain sphere. Later on the husband in turn passes into spirit life, but goes to occupy a realm lower than that of his wife. But the mutual attraction still exists, and so the wife takes up her life in the lower sphere in order to be with her husband and to help him in his progression. Thus they will be enabled to advance together and remain together for all time, or until such other circumstances arise as will cause a natural severance of their present ties.

There are many selfless souls here who have done and are doing the very same thing. They are perfectly free to make their own choice in the matter. The greater happiness, generally speaking, that would be theirs in the higher state, receives some measure of compensation in their being re-united with some much-loved relation or friend.

So you will see, there are no sad partings, no dispersals of pleasantly situated little communities of relations or friends by the natural procedure of spiritual progression. We do not experience that crushing, almost over-whelming depression that you can experience upon the earth at the departure of one who is greatly loved.

Even if a cherished friend has departed into higher regions, and we should feel ourselves becoming saddened by the event, it must be remembered that we are in instantaneous touch with each other here. A thought sent out will bring back the absent one in a twinkling to our side, if that should be the only remedy for our desolation. But that would be an extreme case, a highly improbable eventuality, and scarcely ever to be encountered. Then again, we are unerringly in touch with each other here by thought in ways that I will explain to you later.

As I have had occasion to remark previously, the spirit world is not a static world. There is always movement, especially among its people. How, otherwise, could we eventually pass to the higher states if it were not so? At some time or another certain small communities of a few friends or kindred souls, who are occupying the same domicile together and working in concert, must come under the influence of the universal law of change that is one of the great elements of spirit life. But, these re-groupings, with their consequent severance of earlier ties, are not terrible tragedies. They are the natural outcome of the march of progression. We must move onwards as the will to move exerts itself within us. None would hold us back, although we might elect to stay until other circumstances prevail. But you can be sure of this: we are all completely satisfied under this scheme of things, we know that no other plan would be feasible, and, what is most important from the point of view of our feelings in the matter, we are supremely happy under it.

In my references to the countryside, I have mentioned rivers. How do they flow? They flow in exactly the same manner as do earthly rivers. They begin their life as a small stream, perhaps as a little trickling brook, and they flow on and on becoming deeper and broader in their passage, and finally they flow into the sea. There is nothing very remarkable in that, but the rivers themselves are very remarkable when they are compared with earthly rivers. The rivers of the spirit world are never fast-flowing streams, muddy looking, or heavy in appearance. Nor are unsightly buildings to be found upon their banks, with merchant vessels of all shapes and sizes and degrees of disrepair alongside dingy wharves. However picturesque the ships may be, we have no need for them here, and so they do not exist. Boats of all sorts we do have, but not of the description that I have just mentioned. And we do not have unpleasant factory buildings spoiling the beautiful riverside scenery. Instead, we have magnificent edifices built of spirit world materials such as you are already familiar with, reposing along the waterside, with spacious embankments and splendidly laid-out gardens through which the river threads its placid way, slowly, very slowly, and calmly. When I first saw one of the spirit-world rivers, so slowly was it moving that to my unaccustomed eyes I felt sure that it was not moving at all! But it is possible to see the movement and to feel it.

You can have no conception how glorious it is to glide along such a river in some graceful boat, passing through the rolling banks of flowers upon either hand, or through some peaceful meadow where the trees reflect their shapely forms in the tranquil waters; or again, to draw alongside some beautiful broad marble steps, to go ashore, mount to a greater height and view the ribbon of scintillating colour that the river reveals itself to be from this higher elevation; or, yet again, to proceed up some sequestered backwater to find one's self in the midst of a friend's garden.

Nothing can possibly convey to you the brilliance of the colour, always the colour, that seems to abound in such full measure in the neighbourhood of the rivers. Perhaps it is that the streams themselves reflect back so much colourful light from the flowers that this effect of seeming preponderance of colour is produced. Whatever it may be, we all feel the same about it, and for that reason the rivers always have a very great attraction to the folk in their leisure moments.

The water is of the purest, as you know, but its most remarkable feature, in the opinion of so many of us here, is the ability it has of changing its colours and shades of colours. At times, I have seen the river which runs near my home to be nothing less in appearance than a ribbon of molten gold. All the different hues that are usually reflected in a thousand different ways, appeared to have vanished and in their place was liquid gold. At other times I have seen it shining as though of burnished silver. This rather unusual phenomenon puzzled me considerably in my early days here, but my invaluable friend, Edwin, soon instructed me in such matters as these. The explanation was simple enough. It was just that some visitant from higher realms was, or had been, in the neighbourhood, and the influence which he brought with him was being reflected in the mirror surface of the water. As the influence became absorbed into the immediate surroundings, the river gradually resumed its customary appearance.

I only mention this small incident to show you how these realms of the spirit world are ever affording us some delight or another, unasked—which makes the enjoyment of it still more precious to us.

Akin to the rivers of the spirit world are, of course, the seas. They are like the seas of the earth merely as a body of water, but in no other respect. The waters of the rivers here, and the seas into which they flow, are of the same elements; that is to say, the water is what is known on earth as fresh water. As far as I was able to observe I could not trace the presence of any salt in the sea.

In general appearance there is not a great deal of difference between the rivers and the ocean. Each has the same brilliance of colour, but the rivers by virtue of the fairly close proximity of their banks, with the large masses of flowers and the elegant buildings which adorn them, will have more colours to reflect in their surfaces, and so they will appear to be more colourful. But it must not be presumed that the sea lacks a full measure of colour. Very far from it. No water, wherever situated here, lacks colour. And the sea is never empty of the signs of life. There are always vessels of one sort or another to be seen sailing upon it or riding at anchor. In addition, however far one may travel one is scarcely ever out of sight of an enchantingly lovely island, upon which one is at liberty to wander to one's heart's content, and enjoy the special features which all these islands possess.

One of the islands, of which I have spoken to you before, contains a veritable paradise of bird-life, where some of the most beautiful specimens of birds in all the glory of their gorgeous plumage are to be seen at close hand. They are not segregated and confined in cages, of course, but they are free to pursue their life in their natural element, the air, or to remain upon the ground in the absolute certainty of their complete security from harm. Consequently, they are the friends of any of us who may visit their special domain.

This particular island is another favourite pleasure spot with us, and often do we go there to sit on the soft grass while birds of every description of vivid plumage and of every size come gathering round us, not for food, as one would imagine on earth, but just to demonstrate their knowledge that no harm can come to them, and to express their friendliness with all mankind in these realms. We are such regular visitors there that we know a great many of the birds by sight and by name, for someone is bound to give them names!

Of course bird-life is not confined solely to this one island; indeed, the birds are flying about throughout these and other realms. Just as with you on earth, so are they here with us—'abroad and everywhere'.

I have not visited all the seas of the spirit world, but there is plenty of time yet. My visitations to the seaside have been chiefly to that ocean which is nearest to our particular quarter of these realms.

When viewed from an elevation that is fairly high above sea-level, the water presents a scintillating expanse of colour. There are no storms to agitate the surface violently, at the same time the sea is not always of a glassy smoothness. The gentlest of breezes will play lightly upon the waters, rippling the surface and forming little waves which take on a hundred tints in the smallest space, so that these rays of reflected light are for all the world like the flashes of colour that are to be seen issuing from the purest of diamonds.

It is a thrilling experience to behold for the first time this glittering effect that is natural to all water in the spirit world. When I first beheld it I could hardly believe my eyes so unbelievably inspiring was the spectacle. And even now, although I have become to some extent a seasoned resident of these realms, I can still be thrilled by the interplay of colour whenever I come within sight of river or lake or sea. And that applies to all of us here. Familiarity has not made us indifferent. There would be something radically wrong with ourselves if it did.

There are many fine vessels to be seen upon all the

waters of these regions, many of them the homes of residents. Ownership of such boats, in fact, of any boat, is governed by the same law that applies to all ownership in spirit lands, the law that makes it a *sine qua non* that all our possessions must be earned before we can own them. As far as the smaller craft are concerned, the type which would be known as private river-craft on earth, many people have such boats and spend their leisure moments upon the water, just as do you on earth, but without any of the restrictions or dangers, even, that are to be encountered on earth. It is perfectly safe here for a small child to sail out in a boat entirely alone.

What is the difference, you might wish to ask, between country life and town life in the spirit world? In the form in which that question is framed there is doubtless the impression that life in the spirit world consists of a regularly recurring series of episodes, or functions, dividing life into a number of compartments, as it were, though the compartments themselves might be contiguous. That is how life is composed, more or less, upon earth. So to answer that question, I must place one or two considerations before you.

Your life upon earth is dominated by two factors at least, both of which are unavoidable. They are the need for rest through sleep, and the need for food. To maintain your life at all upon earth, you must provide for these two requirements. As you know, in the spirit world we need neither physical rest nor food. Your life is therefore punctuated by recurring periods of sleeping and eating. A certain part of your life is spent with darkness upon earth, and although you may illuminate the darkness with artificial light, the darkness still remains elsewhere.

In these realms, as you know, too, we have no

darkness at all, *at any time*. Our life, then, is one of absolute continuity in perpetual natural light. We have no blank period in our physical life such as you have during your sleep. We are for ever awake. We carry on with our work until such time as we wish to stop, and then we stop. We can follow on with other work of a different nature, or we can betake ourselves to some form of amusement or entertainment, or we can indulge in our own particular pastime. At the conclusion of the latter, or at such time as we see fit, we will resume our work. Further, we live in a state of perpetual summer; we have no long summer or long winter evenings alternating.

You have no possible means of experiencing these various factors upon earth because they do not and cannot exist there. You must therefore call your imagination into play and try to picture to yourself the particular conditions which I have just outlined to you. You should then be able to see that there is really no difference between town and country life in the spirit world.

The cities of the earth are mere concentrations for reasons of commercial convenience. There being no commerce in the spirit world we have no need for such concentrations. But what has been done is to place all the great halls of learning of these particular realms in one locality. There is no pressing need that they should be so disposed; with equal facility they could have been distributed throughout a wide area of these regions. But it was felt that a number of magnificent buildings, such as are the halls of learning, would present a much more imposing appearance if they were arranged in an orderly plan, each within a moderately close distance of the other. We can think of no better arrangement. And so the buildings were erected many aeons ago. They occupy an immense area of ground, and each is standing in gardens and grounds of peerless beauty. Exactly in the centre of this group of buildings is a temple of unsurpassed grandeur. It forms the hub of the city, and from it radiate all other buildings of whatever nature.

We have no streets as you know them, for we do not require them, but we have broad, spacious thoroughfares of the softest grass upon which to walk. There is no traffic of vehicles here so that there is no necessity for special pavements upon each side of the roadway, as you have for your own security. Sometimes these broad walks are paved with some of the wonderful stone creations of these realms, but more often they are covered with grass.

When you come to view the countryside here you find that without hedges and walls and other boundary marks, the whole landscape becomes one vast expanse of parklands interspersed with rivers and streams and wooded land. Standing amid all these beauties are the dwellings of the inhabitants of these regions of the spirit world, and in a part of the countryside there stands what we call the city. Where one ends and the other begins, it would be difficult to say. There are no municipal or civic rights to be considered, no parochial boundaries to be thought of, no suburban or rural privileges to intervene in any way. The city is part of the countryside; the countryside is part of the city. The life of one is the life of the other, simply because of the continuity of existence in the spirit world, and because of the perpetual day-time and perpetual summer-time. There is no hot and stuffy city to make a visit into the country air so pressing. There is no great commercial attraction of the city to draw folk towards that centre. So that, in effect, the country and the city are one.

I promised, a little while since, that I would speak to you upon the subject of thought. Now, I think, would be a favourable opportunity to do so, leaving for the time such other matters of spirit life that are worthy of discussion.

III

SPIRIT PERSONALITY

When the spirit world is described as being a world of thought, where thought is the great creative power, and where thought is concrete and perceivable by all men, the conclusion is very often erroneously drawn that the spirit world is an unsubstantial place, and that we, its inhabitants, are vague shadowy people, lacking any real substance, and answering for all purposes to that very earthly designation of 'ghosts'! Pursuing this mistaken deduction, the life of the spirit world people must inevitably be somewhat dream-like and illusive.

The incarnate think along these lines because to them thought is something that can be practised unseen and unheard. On earth thought is secret to the thinker until such time as he wishes to give verbal or other expression to his thoughts. It is customary to say on earth: our thoughts are our own; we can think what we like; thoughts can never harm anyone, and so on. So that when we of the spirit world assert that our world is a world of thought, the incarnate immediately revert to their own thoughts and their unsubstantial nature, and thereupon place the spirit world in the same category of tenuous things.

Generally speaking, upon earth thought must have some form of concrete expression for it to be effective. The architect must first think of his cathedral, or whatever it may be, commit his thoughts to paper in regular order and with exactitude before the builder can make any commencement upon the outward and visible expression of his original thoughts. And so it is with a multitude of other things, from the simplest article to the most complicated instrument or ornate building. On earth thought must have a medium of some sort before it can find the slightest trace of outward expression. For this reason, among others, the incarnate are prone to regard the earth as being the one certain and substantial world in which it is possible to exist. The spirit world becomes the very opposite.

The incarnate do not realise the force and power of thought or else they would never think along such lines as I have indicated. Every thought that passes with force and purpose through the mind of an earth dweller is projected from his mind as a thought-form. To speak unscientifically, it is registered, at least for a time, upon the surrounding ether. It depends, of course, upon the thought itself, and of what it consists. If it is merely one of those passing thoughts that all folk upon earth have in their minds at various moments during the day, then such thoughts will be registered in the manner I have just indicated. If the thought is directed towards some friend who is now resident in the spirit world, that thought, if it is properly directed with purpose and intent, will inevitably reach that friend. It will reach him or her just as it is sent, no more and no less good or bad or indifferent.

Thought may be invisible to the majority of earth dwellers but it is very much visible to spirit folk. People who are still on earth, and whose psychic powers have been developed, are often capable of seeing these thought-forms. That ability raises problems which sometimes lead to mistakes and misunderstandings.

Thought is upon a different plane, a higher plane of

existence from that organ of the earthly body, the brain, through which thought functions on earth. Thought is upon the same plane of existence as the mind, and the mind belongs truly to the spirit world. And by higher plane I do not mean a higher spiritual plane, but one that cannot be observed by the ordinary physical organs of perception. In the spirit world thought has direct and instantaneous action upon whatsoever it is directed, whether it be upon a human being or upon what on earth is called 'an inanimate object'. (I cannot use the latter term appositely in connection with spirit world objects, because all objects, all things, have life, certain and unmistakable. There is no such state as that of being lifeless in the spirit world.) It is not until you come into the spirit world that you really know just what thought can do. And I do assure you, my good friend, that some of us are positively horrified when we find out for the first time!

In the spirit world thoughts do not become visible immediately upon their passing through a person's mind. They are not flying about in a loose fashion. The idle thoughts of which I spoke travel no further than your immediate earthly surroundings. Thoughts directed to some friend in the spirit world will reach that friend, and they cannot be classed as loose thoughts.

Imagine to yourself the state of confusion, of congestion almost, and of embarrassment if all our thoughts in the spirit world were visible. But because they are not immediately visible, that is not to say that they are not potent, for assuredly they are very potent. No, they are not visible as you regard it, but they will unfailingly reach their destination wherever it may be. If directed towards some friend upon earth, in many cases it is problematical whether the friend will perceive them; or, perceiving them, whether he will know whence they have come. But if our thoughts be directed towards some friend in the spirit world, there will be no such doubt or uncertainty.

How do we receive thoughts in the spirit world? One of the first and most interesting experiments that Ruth and I carried out under the friendly eye of Edwin during our early explorations of these realms, was that of hearing Edwin speak to us from a distance. Without recounting the full circumstances, it is sufficient to say that although Edwin was in sight of us both, yet he was too far away for us to hear his voice even if he had used it above his normal tones. But we both distinctly heard his voice sounding close to our ears. At first, of course, we could not believe our ears, and we were rather inclined to regard the whole thing as some trick or other that Edwin was performing for amusement and general merriment. But he repeated his message to us—it was merely bidding us rejoin him—and it was so unmistakable that we forthwith did as directed.

As a prelude to hearing Edwin's voice, we had both perceived a bright flash to appear before the eyes. It was in no sense blinding or startling; indeed, the flash was too beautiful for that.

And that, I think, describes briefly but precisely what happens to all of us when a thought is passed between one and another of us. The thought is invisible in transit, it arrives at its destination instantaneously, when it manifests itself before us as a pleasant but compelling flash of clear light, and we can then hear the voice of our communicator speaking close to the ear, *as it seems*. I say as it seems, because here I am not attempting to give a scientific explanation of *how* it happens, but confining myself solely to what *does* happen. The voice always sounds to me to be close to the ear, and most people here say that the same thing occurs in their own case. It may be some sort of inner perception of the voice, though to me it always sounds far too like the owner's actual voice for that. My own view is that the sound of the voice actually travels through the air, and that we receive it upon the natural apparatus of our minds.

I confess that I have not looked into the matter in that deep manner that some people, perhaps, will think that I ought to have done, if only for the purpose of supplying them with a long and deep, accurate and scientific explanation of the whole process. But I am persuaded that the majority of my good friends will much rather have this frankly and obviously unscientific description of what takes place here— during every second of time, just as a matter of course, than that I should lead them into some deep morass of scientific disquisition from which we should all have some difficulty in extricating ourselves!

I do not profess to a knowledge of science, and I always feel that while we are peering deeply into causes and detailed explanations we are missing all the beauties of the very thing we are examining.

There is so much here that we take for granted, that is to say, we take things as they present themselves, without demanding learned explications of them. And it is the same with you who are still upon earth. Suppose, for example, I were to ask you (supposing, also, that I did not already know) how you managed to move yourself upon your two legs in the common feat of walking. I think it would much more suit your taste for you to tell me briefly just what you did with your legs and how tired they can become after prolonged activity, than to treat me to an erudite essay upon the various muscles of the leg, their names, their shape and size, their exact mode of action, their particular function, and so on. In the meantime, while the legs were being thus dilated upon, the friend, whom the two legs were supporting, was passing through some charming country, a description of which would be so much more entertaining!

And so it is with a great many other matters here—here in my world and in your world too. While science has its important place in both our worlds, yet we do not ponder every minute of our lives upon the inner working of the numberless functions of men and things that constitute life in either world. Science must have its proper position, but life would be rather dull and dreary, and certainly rather complicated, if we paused to inquire into the various modes of operation of so many common actions. We must just take things as they are. That is your general attitude upon earth; that is our general attitude here in the spirit world.

My chief purpose is to give you as many details as possible or practicable of our life in spirit lands. To state a fact as plainly as possible, to provide explanations only where necessary to an intelligent understanding of my account, and to leave it to others to probe more deeply into causes, must be my aim.

When thought is directed to us from the earth it takes the same form of a flash before the eyes. There is no difference whatever in the actual process. It matters not whence the thought has been directed, whether from your world of the earth or as an inter-communication in the spirit world. The process is universal, and there are no variations in it.

When I spoke to you, a moment ago, of the thought-forms you create in the ether immediately surrounding you on earth by your having idle thoughts in your mind, that must not be taken as also applying to us in the spirit world. If it did the spirit world would be a strange place, and the people in it would appear stranger still, for they would continually seem to be enveloped either in a kind of haze of thought-forms or something even more substantial.

The case is different with people on earth. That part of the spirit world which is immediately inter-penetrating your world, that is to say, the invisible world in the immediate vicinity of the particular spot, for example, where you are reading these words, this spot is not part of the realms of light. It is dark. It may have its minute patches of light in certain well-defined places, but the greater part of it is dark. Thought, of the kind that contains no evil within it, will be bright, and therefore it will show up in the surrounding gloom, just as the light of a tiny flame will illumine the gloom of a chamber from which all other light is excluded. Even a limited diffusion of light will be the case. But take the tiny flame into the bright light of the sun and the diffusion seems to end, the feeble light having become absorbed by the greater light of the sun. The flame will still be visible, but its light will be strictly limited to its source.

This somewhat elementary analogy will serve, I hope, to illustrate the difference between thought in the in visible regions closely adjacent to your world, and thought as it is in these bright realms where I live. Even this simple analogy must be qualified by saying that however wandering may be our thoughts they are not visible like the flame of light in the sunshine. Things are far better ordered than that in the spirit world! We do have mental privacy here. Without it social intercourse would be trying, to say the least. We are living in a land of truth, that is certain; but we do not carry things to such an extreme that we must voice the truth openly upon all occasions. As with you, so with us; there are moments and occasions when silence is golden!

But it is essential that one should learn to think properly as an inhabitant of the spirit world. One of the first things one has to do here, as a new arrival, is to think properly. It is not a difficult achievement, and not nearly so formidable a task as it may sound. It concerns one's thought about people rather than thoughts of a general nature upon things. When thought is concerned with a person, the thought, if it has sufficient force behind it, will travel to that person. If it happens to be of a pleasant or complimentary description, or of a jovial and genial nature, then the percipient will be happy to receive it. But all thoughts are not of this innocuous sort, and our mental secrets may have passed out of our minds only to have found their destination in the very last place we wanted them to be, namely, in the mind of the person of whom we were so freely thinking.

The thought, however, must have a sufficient measure of directive power behind it to send it upon its journey, and this factor is the saving of many of us, because so many thoughts are mere birds of passage in our minds, and while they are there they have little really deep concentration upon the individual concerned. But the very prospect of what can happen is enough to make us keep a strict watch upon our minds, and in a brief period it becomes as second nature to us.

There are many things that we have to unlearn and re-learn when we first come to dwell in spirit lands, but our minds, being then free of a heavy physical brain, are at liberty to exercise their powers to the full. We are enabled, therefore, to acquire rapidly the methods of living under different conditions of existence. Our memories behave as memories should; that's to say, they are not erratic in their retentive performance, but can be relied upon to act perfectly. You can see how invaluable such an attribute will be when it becomes necessary to learn afresh how to do things according to spirit laws. It is in this rapid way that so many common actions quickly become as second nature.

Although, in the spirit world, thought has such direct action and is generally so powerful, that does not mean that thought makes physical effort practically unnecessary, or even undesirable. There are a great many things for our hands to do in the spirit world, and I would add that our feet also are constantly in use! We like to walk, just as we used to upon earth. What could be more natural? We are human beings after all, though some folk would deny us this characteristic. We are human, and we behave in a manner that is human. Our feet were given to us to use, and we walk upon them.

Because we can create so much with our minds, because we can fabricate things by the close application of thought, then, it might be imagined, there is precious little left for our hands to do, except to make up our full complement of limbs, and so obviate our presenting ourselves as something of monstrosities. The truth is that we use our hands in a thousand different actions during what you would call the day's work, or during a day in our life.

Think for a moment. Recall the scores of instances in which one may use the hands. For example, in our spirit homes we pick up a book, we open or close a door, we shake hands with some friend who calls; we arrange some flowers upon the table; we paint a picture, or play upon a musical instrument; or we may operate scientific apparatus of some sort. Such instances could be multiplied a thousandfold, and would become too tedious for words in their enumeration. We like to employ our hands in conjunction with our minds as well as exercising our minds alone, just as do you on earth. People take a natural delight in fashioning objects by hand, and so allowing the mind to work through their hands. There are plenty of things that could be created in these realms purely by thought and without the least interposition of the hands, but we like to go the long way round sometimes and find some employment for our hands, and we relish the enjoyment that comes from it.

But occasions do arise when we act quickly, in fact, instantaneously. We wish to go to a particular place in the realms which is, say, hundreds of miles distant, as distances are reckoned on earth. We could walk the entire distance without a trace of fatigue, but in such cases we prefer a speedier form of transportation. We therefore abandon the slow walking method of locomotion, and we bring our minds to bear upon the matter. By direct action of the mind we find ourselves instantaneously in the very place in which we wished to be.

As to how we think ourselves in a certain place, here again I would not offer you a scientific explanation for reasons which I have given you, so I will confine myself to this: in the spirit world our bodies are under complete control by our minds. The former do just that which the latter wishes or commands. A wish becomes a command in this case. Now with you, your mind may wish to be in a certain place, and no matter how hard you may wish it, you are entirely at the mercy of your physical body. You may even sit in your chair and imagine yourself, in every detail of circumstances, in the precise place. You can 'see' yourself there, but the physical body must go too if you desire to be there physically. And that may raise all sorts of problems which will come readily enough to your mind— opportunity, for example; or the requisite time and means for getting to the desired destination. These are all considerations affecting the physical body, because you must take that with you, for in the physical body is the brain, and it is through the brain that the mind works. This is the natural and normal order of things on earth.

In the spirit world it is very different. We have no heavy physical body. The body which we possess is in every respect equal to our minds. Our minds have no heavy vehicle by or through which they have to function. Thinking is at once translated into action, but without the intermedium of a physical brain such as you know it. The brain which is resident within our heads is not as your physical brain; our bodies are not as your physical bodies. With us our whole being, our limbs, our muscles and so forth, are completely subservient to the mind in so far as their acting according to our will is concerned. For the rest, our bodies are subservient to the natural laws of the spirit world.

We also perform certain actions subconsciously in exactly the same way as do you. For example, we breathe in precisely the same way as you breathe. Our hearts beat in a fashion exactly similar to yours, and they are subject to the same subconscious maintenance in their beating. But we have that which you do not have, namely, complete and absolute mastery of the muscles of our limbs. When we come to learn some new art, or endeavour to become proficient in some task that requires the mastery by the brain over the muscles, then you can see just how perfect is the attunement of our minds with our muscles. It is not really a mastery of the one over the other, although I have expressed it in that way. To be more accurate, it is an absolute attunement, the one with the other.

Now with you on earth, the effort of walking makes imperative the use of various muscles. First, you have a heavy body to move along the ground on which you are standing, and you have certain laws of gravity which are pulling you towards that ground. The gravity is so adjusted that your feet will fall to the ground easily without requiring any effort to push them down. The matter is nicely balanced. When your legs are tired after prolonged use they will fall the more readily to the ground than when you are fresh. Who upon earth has not experienced at some time or another that great heaviness of the limbs consequent upon fatigue? It is one of our constant joys that we never suffer from such disabilities. There is a law of gravity here in the spirit world, but we are not subservient to it. All else is, but we human beings are not so. Or to put it another way, our minds can and do at all times rise above it. That again is second nature to us. If we should tumble down, we cannot hurt ourselves because our spirit bodies are impervious to all injury in whatever shape or form.

Incidentally, we do not often fall because we have not the heavy and rather clumsy bodies that are essential upon earth. It is mostly newly-arrived folk who do the tumbling! When we have become fully acquainted with the power and force of our minds we never do such awkward things!

I am afraid this must seem rather a long way towards answering the question as to how we move ourselves instantaneously from one place to another, but you know how simple questions demand the consideration of other factors not unconnected with the original question in order to make the answer to the latter intelligible. Hence, therefore, my seeming deviation and protractedness.

The laws of gravity will keep all the 'inanimate objects' of the spirit world in the place where they properly belong—the buildings, the rivers, the sea, and the rest. It will keep us there, too, but only in the qualified sense that I have just mentioned to you. Remember that on earth your mind is limited in certain directions by the abilities—or disabilities—of the physical body. If, say, you wish to write something down, your hand and your arm must be in a fit condition to do so. The same rule applies to the rest of your body. To walk, your legs and feet, and indeed, many other parts of the body, must be in a moderately sound state to do so. The speed at which your limbs can move is not limited by the wishes of the mind, but by the ability of the limbs to move. The performer upon a musical instrument knows how true this is from the unremitting practice which he has perforce to do before his hands can travel at the speed which the music makes necessary.

In the spirit world our bodies are always in a state of absolute perfection of condition. The muscles and the various parts of our bodies will respond as instantly and as rapidly as we wish the moment we set the thought in motion. We set the thought in motion, the thought sets the limbs and its parts in motion. There is no lagging, no perceptible fraction of a moment between our thought and its action. It will recall to your mind the familiar phrase: to think is to act. That is literally what takes place in the spirit world. Some of our actions are subconscious, as I have indicated to you; breathing, for example. We do not have to learn how to do that.

My mention of breathing has brought me to a point in our discussion where I think it would be acceptable if I were to speak to you upon the subject of what we both know as the spirit body. There are particular aspects about it upon which one of my friends upon earth has expressed the wish for further information. I am happy to give it to the best of my ability, but I would limit myself, as I have done throughout the whole of these writings, to knowledge which has been gained by my own experience. My reason for the latter is simply that it could be reasonably inferred that I might have recourse to the many books of learning upon all subjects that are to be found within the library of the great hall of learning. In effect, I should merely have to 'look things up' in any work devoted to the subject under consideration. I have recounted to you how we have the truth here reposing between the covers of thousands of volumes. One has only to consult these, it might be said, to become possessed of an immensity of knowledge upon all subjects under the sun. Thus one could soon ascertain the literal truth upon so many of the questions that have puzzled generations of students and inquirers. The truth is there in those books, certainly, but information of a highly technical nature is not to be gleaned merely for the reading. We must understand something—in many cases a good deal—of our subject before we can plunge into technicalities which a full exposition of the truth will disclose. I must, therefore, know and understand my subject before I can pass on the information and knowledge with any hope of *your* understanding it. How, otherwise, am I to know that I have given you the correct answer to a question? It is the only satisfactory course to you, who have followed me so patiently thus far, and to me, that I should know what I am talking about, and so give you only those things of which I have specific knowledge or experience.

I have hitherto always tried to make it clear when I am only expressing a personal opinion, and when I am quoting from the knowledge and experience of my friends in the spirit world.

And now let us proceed with our friend's question. My friend of the earth recalls my account of the orchestral concert which I attended here, and he says that 'if people play wind instruments in the spirit world, they must have lungs that are capable of breathing air.' And so he asks: 'Do people breathe in the spirit world? If so, are the lungs used for oxygenating the blood?'

Such reasoning is perfectly accurate. The spirit world has air just as you have on earth, and we have lungs in our bodies with which to breathe it. And it does 'oxygenate' the blood in what would be the spirit world equivalent of that process. Upon earth the air you breathe will help to purify the blood. In the spirit world we have good rich blood running through our veins, and we breathe the beautiful clean fresh fragrant air, but while your blood undergoes the process of oxygenating, our blood is *reinvigorated* by the spiritual force and energy that is one of the principal constituents of the air we breathe here.

Could one exist without it? Hardly. It gives us a measure of life-force just as it does you on earth. But you could not exist upon air alone. You must have food and drink. We do not need these two latter commodities, as you know, but we derive another part of our sustenance from the light of these realms, from the abundance of colour, from the water, from the fruit when we wish to eat of it, from the flowers, and from all that is beautiful itself. As these realms positively abound in beauty you will see why we enjoy such perfect health.

But we also take in strength from the great spiritual force that is being constantly poured down upon us all from the Father of Heaven Himself. It is, as it were, an eternal magnetic current that is for ever charging us with force and power, and giving us life.

It really comes to this, that we derive our life-force from a score of different sources; sources, moreover, that we do not have to seek as do you with your food and drink, but which literally envelope us wherever we go, whatever we do. We cannot shut ourselves off from the means of life, nor can the means of life be denied us or ever fail us here. The air we breathe cannot become polluted, nor can the water become in a similar state of impurity.

The earthly body is so constituted that through various processes and natural functions a firm resistance is made to the onslaught of germs that cause disease. When it is behaving normally and properly such disease will be successfully repelled. But even though the earthly body should successfully resist disease, the potential causes of it, the germs, still remain in the earth world. In the spirit world there are no such things as germs of any description, therefore there can be no disease of any sort whatever. Moreover, the spirit body is completely impervious to any kind of injury. It cannot be damaged by accident, and it is imperishable and incorruptible. So that whatever organs we possess they can never become disordered in the slightest degree. We are constantly enjoying a state of *perfect* health, upon which there are no two opinions among all of us here in these realms. The slightest trace of ache or pain is something not only unheard of, but from our point of view, *fantastically impossible.*

It is obvious from what I have told you that one or two organs of the earthly body would be manifestly superfluous in the spirit body. We do not eat food because we are never hungry. There is therefore no waste that has to be eliminated from our bodies as is essential with your physical bodies. The food that you eat goes through its processes, after you have consumed it, to provide what is necessary for the physical body, until it finally becomes waste matter. And to perform this series of actions various organs are vital.

We possess an interior mechanism which follows much upon the same lines as does yours, but there is this supreme difference, namely, that we have no waste matter that must be eliminated from the body. There is no such thing as waste matter in these realms. That which is not wanted either ceases to exist altogether, or is returned to the source whence it came. By ceasing to exist, I do not mean that which is not wanted is annihilated, but that it ceases to exist in the form it held *before* it became unwanted. Perhaps you will recall an amusing experience which I had shortly after my arrival here. I told you how astonished I was to find that the juice which had poured from some fruit that I was eating, and had, so I thought, run down my clothing, had, in fact, done nothing of the sort. *It had completely disappeared.* All that had happened in this case was simply that the juice of the fruit had returned to the tree whence the fruit had come. That is the explanation I was given, and that is what we all know to occur in any other circumstances of a similar nature. If you ask me *how* it happens, then, perforce, I will say honestly that I do not know. Lest my ignorance should appear too great that I should ever set myself to inform others, let me hasten to add that there is no one in these realms who could provide an explanation upon this point. There is no esoteric secret about it that such information should be withheld from us. It is just that our spiritual evolution has not proceeded sufficiently far for us to understand if we were told. What we cannot yet understand ourselves, it is impossible for us to expound for your understanding.

The organs that we possess, therefore, have their very definite purpose for their existence. We do not carry about with us organs that are redundant. Their purpose is to act as a channel for the life-force, the etheric power, if you wish to call it so, that emanates from a multiplicity of sources. There is no fear that some organs, or all of them, will become atrophied because they do not seem to be employed in the same manner as their counterparts in the earthly body. The organs of assimilation of the earthly body will become seriously affected if a sufficient quantity of food is not passed through them. No such situation could arise in our spirit bodies, because the lifeforce here amply sustains them and keeps them in proper working order, and thus they fulfil their objects.

The spirit body, then, possesses only such organs as are vital to it, and they can be regarded as a modification of their earthly counterparts. The further significance of this will be plainer to you when I tell you that, with the exception of the higher and highest realms, the spirit world, in which millions upon millions of us are living, is populated entirely from the earth, and from no other source. Procreation belongs to the earth, and has no place in the spirit world.

It has become a habit to begin the counting of time by some supposed date of the creation of the world. Time, in its measured sense, can be said to have commenced with the formation of the earth, but human life was already in existence long before then. The spirit world was long in existence before the earth, but the spirit world was not empty. It was inhabited by great souls whose knowledge and wisdom and spiritual progression and evolution have been proceeding steadily throughout the whole of this colossal period of time. All these beings possess a body which in its parts and its functions are exactly similar to the body of any one of us here, regardless of our position upon the ladder of spiritual progression, though, under certain conditions, that body would appear outwardly to us infinitely lesser beings as a blaze of light.

The spirit body which we all possess is the normal body. The earthly body, which temporarily covers the spirit body during its earthly passage, is a modification of the spirit body, an accommodation to earthly laws and conditions and modes of life. The life of the individual begins upon earth, it spends a limited period in that sphere, and then comes to us in the spirit world. The personality and individuality and attributes of the person are in their initial stages of formation upon earth, and the process is continued after his arrival in the spirit world.

The physical distinctions of race will be preserved, borne upon his face, in the very colour of his skin, and in other ways that will readily occur to you, and these he will retain in the spirit world.

The true sphere of life is the spirit world because it is permanent. The spirit world is therefore the standard of life as it is ultimately to be for us all, and so the spirit body, not the earthly body, is the standard of the human form.

In company with many others, I have seen and spoken to at least one illustrious being whose period of life, in years, reaches astronomical figures. He possesses, just as do you or I, the ordinary normal complement of limbs; he has hair upon his head. His hands, anatomically like yours and mine, have their full number of finger-nails. And so we might go on, through the complete catalogue of the parts of the human anatomy as it exists in the spirit world. The exalted nature of his being and the elevated realm in which he resides make him no different, anatomically, from the rest of us. His spirituality and wisdom and knowledge are, of course, in their high degree incomparable with us here. But we are not considering that for the moment. What we are considering is that when man, who has lived upon earth, comes to the spirit world to continue his life here, he sheds with his earthly body all such organs of that body as will be superfluous in his new mode of living. The organs with which he now finds himself are for ever beyond harm of every description. No germ can attack the body; no destructive force can exert the slightest influence upon it. It is incorruptible. Its various organs, such as the heart and lungs, act *perfectly*. For example, the beating of the heart remains constant and normal under all conditions. We cannot *literally* become breathless. (I have sometimes said that some particular experience has left me breathless almost, but this is a figure of speech only.) Our respiration, like the action of the heart, remains always at its normal rate. And so it is throughout the rest of our bodies.

I do not pretend to the knowledge of a physician or a surgeon, but I do know that my body functions perfectly, that I enjoy, as we all enjoy, a state of perfect health such as I never for one moment enjoyed during my life on earth. Indeed, it is impossible to know what absolute, perfect health can be until one comes to live here in the spirit world. The body I possess is not a hollow drum, a mere empty vessel in the ownership of which I am able, in some mysterious fashion, to carry on my life. There is good rich blood flowing through my veins. There is no doubt about that, for I can observe the flesh-pink tinge it gives to my skin, as it does to us all. We have the complexions of healthy individuals, though the former may vary in the depth of their colour by virtue of the various racial characteristics which you can easily call to mind. Whatever may be the precise shade of our complexions or of our skin in general, we none of us have the pallor that is usually associated either with a poor state of health or with some particular form of earthly occupation.

The circulation of the blood within our bodies is the means of diffusing the vital force that keeps us alive. If you should ask me why it should be necessary to have these organs to do this work, then I can only say that it is impossible for me to explain the fact of human creation itself. We might ask in turn, why does the incarnate person have his organs to do such work as is required of them? We should have to go to the very beginning and ask why has man come to be in the form that is familiar to us, and not in some other form. We must take things as they are in this instance at least. To do otherwise is rather to suggest that we could make several improvements upon the anatomy of our bodies were we given the opportunity. As far as we, in the spirit world, are concerned *no* improvement could possibly be made upon the structure and operation of our spirit bodies.

And I think that in these very bodies we have at least one assured example of perfection in our midst, and which we enjoy now. The greater perfection—I use this phrase in accordance with the terms of our previous discussion upon perfection—the greater perfection that awaits us when we proceed to a higher realm is a spiritual perfection, and will not apply to the state of health of our bodies. We may feel so much lighter, more etherealized, more rarefied, but as far as I have been able to ascertain, we shall feel in a precisely similar state of buoyant, brilliant health as we do now in these realms.

It is manifestly impossible for me to take every organ of the body and deal with its particular functions in due order. What we can do, to sum up the matter briefly, is to reflect upon this: the spirit body is possessed of organs that are proper to it and to the world in which it carries out its functions. The earthly body will answer to the same description in its own sphere of action. The spirit body, coming first in the order of 'creation', is the standard of human form and figure. The earthly body resembles it, but it has certain other organs added by which it carries out certain processes that are essential to its continued survival upon earth. The two principals of these processes are the means of assimilating food and the means of perpetuating human life upon earth. Food we do not need in the spirit world, and the population of spirit lands is derived, with the exception of those beings in the higher and highest realms to which I have referred, entirely from the earth in so far as this spirit universe is concerned. In discarding my earthly body at my physical dissolution, I found that my spirit body was without certain organs, the possession of which would be entirely redundant. Such organs have no counterpart in or upon the spirit body.

A question may naturally be asked as to how we can live with some of our organs missing. The answer is that they are not missing; they were never there! The spirit body performs perfectly because it is perfectly constructed, complete in all its parts, and only possesses such organs as it requires—in number slightly less than those required by the earthly body.

Now we come to another question from our same good friend, which is away altogether from the contemplation of our bodies and concerns the intellectual side of life here. He asks in effect: 'How is it that a person who was a clergyman during his earthly life and who was a firm upholder of his church's teachings and of what is orthodox in religious matters – how is it that such a person can, in communicating with the earth, give every sign imaginable of having quickly thrown off his religious beliefs and his orthodoxy?'

The same question could apply to a large number of people in a greater or less degree according to the views which they held upon earth. Orthodoxy is not the only thing that can mentally and intellectually shackle a being on earth.

Religious beliefs, both orthodox and unorthodox, can exert a most powerful hold upon the minds of human beings. The former, in general, are too widely known to need amplification, but of the latter, the unorthodox, there are many forms. A great many people hold that a firm belief in a book of ancient chronicles, without even remotely understanding a tithe of its contents, is fully sufficient to assure them of a safe journey to 'the next world', and the certainty of a residence in some salubrious spot among the 'elect'.

Some people hold that a staunch belief in the merits of another will achieve the same results. Whatever form these beliefs take, they are most of them of the crudest description, and upon arrival in the spirit world, the ardent upholders of the childish creeds discover their true worth—which is precisely *nothing*. Now it is exactly according to the mental and intellectual make-up of an individual when he arrives in the spirit world as to how long it will take him to shake off the erroneous beliefs and mistaken ideas which he has accumulated during his life on earth. The person with an 'open mind', provided that mind is not too 'open' and therefore too easily swayed in one direction after another without perceiving the truth, such a person will the more quickly see what his new life involves in the matter of altered outlook. If he is ready to throw off the old life at once and take up the new life with equal celerity, then so much the better and happier will that person be.

It is possible of achievement. Many, many times have Edwin, Ruth, and I witnessed this very thing happening. You can appreciate how we rejoice—and our new friend with us—at this quick awakening to the truth. It is good for us all, and especially it reduces hard work to a minimum. But some people are very stubborn. They will scarcely credit the evidence of their own senses and are therefore not very disposed to place much reliance upon our assurances and asseverations when we try to explain just what the new life means to them. Time will work its usual wonders, and so we are not in any great hurry when we find that an individual appears likely to require some convincing.

To come more specifically to the terms of our friend's question, it depends upon what is meant by *quickly* as regards the time taken by an inhabitant of the spirit world to abandon orthodox religious views. Here we are measuring time in earthly terms. A few hours taken to achieve this end would doubtless seem the extreme of rapidity in which to relinquish beliefs that have been held for a lifetime. But with the right type of mind it could be done; indeed, it has been done on many occasions to which I can bear witness of personal experience.

The age of the new arrival must also be taken into consideration, whether he (or she) be young, middle-aged, or elderly. So you see, there are a number of factors to be taken into account, either singly or in conjunction with each other. There is, for instance, another element which will weigh in the matter: how firmly were the beliefs held? Were they deep-rooted, or merely superficial? People will sometimes make a demonstration of holding certain religious beliefs because they have been brought up in those beliefs from childhood. They may not have bothered to think very much for themselves, and so they have proceeded through their earthly life in an easy fashion religiously, not really caring, but content to follow the rest of the family in their practices. So much for general terms. I can, however, speak from my own personal experience.

During my earthly life I was a clergyman of the orthodox church, but I was not entirely ignorant of the presence around me of an invisible world over which, so it appeared to me, my church had no jurisdiction whatever. My own psychic faculties were not very powerful, but at least they were strong enough for me to disbelieve what my church most emphatically taught in this connexion, namely, that such manifestations as I was permitted to see were all the work of 'the devil'. Now here I could perceive no evidence at all of diabolic intervention. What I did see was decidedly harmless in every way. I therefore frankly disbelieved what the church taught me and told me to teach others upon the subject. But I did not voice this disbelief. That was a secret which I carried with me into the spirit world. I should have done no good had I expressed what I thought openly.

And so I kept these discoveries to myself. Naturally, I believed in a future state of life, and what I saw for myself, psychically, confirmed that belief. Secretly, I differed from the church in its attitude towards such experiences as I had had, but at the same time I chose to consider my own position in the world. The church's hold upon me was a powerful one, and this hold was made the stronger by the absence of greater and wider experiences of a psychic nature such as so many of my friends upon earth are enjoying at this present moment.

I was prepared in my own mind for surprises of considerable magnitude, ready, more or less, to reconstruct my whole outlook, ready, if need be, to jettison my orthodox views in the light of the truth whatever it might be. While I was still upon earth I tried to steer an even course between the little knowledge I had managed to glean of psychic matters concerning the 'afterlife' and the church's teachings.

In my mind the church's teachings weighed more heavily in the scales than did my scanty knowledge of psychic things, but I was fully prepared to find conditions totally different from the 'hereafter' as sketchily touched upon by the church.

I had the great authority—at least, I *thought* it to be great—of the church behind me in whatever religious matters I spoke upon publicly in my preaching; I had no authority behind me in my psychic experiences. Indeed, those to whom I related these experiences at once pronounced me as being tempted by 'the devil'!

Some there are, I dare say, who will say that I should have braved all, pursued my investigations farther and deeper, and abided by the result. The result, they would say, would have been inevitable. I should have discovered that the church's teachings were fundamentally wrong, and then it would have been the right and proper thing for me to renounce the church in favour of the truth as revealed to me through communication with the great spirit world. I wish that I had done so. However, as events have transpired, I have nothing to regret *now*. Through the kind offices of devoted friends and companions I have been enabled to attain to a state of happiness such as I never believed could be possible.

When I had reached the end of my journey upon earth and I found myself at last in the great world upon which I had contemplated so often and so deeply, there to find myself in the very presence of an old friend and colleague who had 'pre-deceased' me by some years, I think it is true to say that I was prepared for anything. Although I had no notion just what it might be. What happened after this meeting I have already set down. It required but 'half an eye' to see that the church was wrong in so much that it had taught me, and which in turn I had taught others. So overwhelmed was I by the beauty of these realms, by the immensity of the splendid prospect that was opening out before me under the able guidance of my friend, Edwin, that I had no difficulty at all in forgetting what the church taught.

An earnest conversation with Edwin was ultimately sufficient to sweep away from my mind all the cobwebs of dogma and creed which had hung about me, and by a simple exposition of the truth to show me that I had not a care in the world if I should so choose to regard the conditions of my new life. The one regret which I felt has since led me back to the earth thus to communicate, and in so doing I have achieved a hundredfold more than I ever dreamed would be possible.

There are many cases parallel to mine. That I know from experience in our work. It is nothing really remarkable, then, that I should so quickly throw off my orthodoxy and become as one with the inhabitants of these sunny realms.

It has been remarked, also, that some of us who come to the earth to speak to our friends, seem to have altered, some of us only slightly, others almost beyond recognition except by such certain evidence as we give of our identity. How is it that we have so changed—for the better, it might be observed?

This apparent transformation of character is explainable by the fact that upon earth there are few people who really show themselves to the world as they truly are.

In ancient days upon earth, folk were in general much simpler in their tastes and their habits and behaviour than they are now. Then they were not afraid to speak their inmost thoughts more openly to one another, provided those thoughts were not of too violent a religious or political nature. People were in many respects more neighbourly in those days when life was simpler. But in these times of greater 'civilization', when the world has become more sophisticated, when people seem less reliant upon each other, dwellers upon earth have withdrawn within themselves until it is difficult to form any very reliable opinion upon the true character of anyone. People are more shy of expressing themselves openly.

The earth, too, has advanced in many directions, making life vastly more complicated. Life is more harassing, it proceeds at a much swifter pace, and a great concentration of energy is crammed into a few hours that would scarcely be spread over the same number of days in olden times.

Now all these conditions bring with them a consequent infirmity of temper. Under stress of such a life we do not always appear at our best. We can become irritable, or cynical; we think we are possessed of all truth, and inclined to regard as fools others who do not think as we do. We become thoroughly intolerant. We may sneer just to give vent to our feelings, and those same feelings may have been induced by something which has gone wrong or not pleased us. We may suffer from poor health of the physical body. We may be overworked or under-worked. We may have too much pleasure or not enough. And so one could go on multiplying causes for our giving exhibitions of character and temperament which are not really our own, which do not come from our 'better selves', to use the old term.

That, broadly speaking, is life on earth as it affects a large number of people. Now let us contemplate the altered state of life upon our coming to the spirit world.

You know by now some few facts concerning life in these lands. As we step into these realms we leave all the worrying cares of the earth behind us. Gone is the poor health we may have had there. Gone, too, are the rush and bustle of earthly life in every department of its complex activities. We do not even need to worry about the state of the weather in these perpetually sunny lands, and that alone, almost, is enough to cheer the heart immeasurably!

Here in the spirit world we stand revealed as we *truly* are. There is no longer any question as to what description of person we are. We can give voice to our thoughts without the fear of being considered foolish, simple, eccentric or childish. We cease to be intolerant here because we find that others are tolerant to us, and there is precious little—indeed, nothing at all—to be intolerant about in these realms. We are a happy community of numberless millions of people, with each one of whom we can be upon the most friendly, genial, and affable of terms, giving and receiving respect to and from every one of our fellows. No single person has ever to endure that which is distasteful to him because there is no one here to cause that which is distasteful to others. The beauties and charms of these realms act like an intellectual tonic; they bring out only that which is and always was the very best in one. Whatever was not the very best in one upon earth will be swamped by the good nature and kindness which the very air here will bring out, like some choice bloom beneath the warm summer sun.

There is no room for the unpleasant phases of human character that are so often exhibited upon earth. They cannot enter these realms. And in so far as such elements of character and temperament as we show upon earth are not the *true* reflection of our real selves, we shall at once cast them aside for ever as we enter the spirit world upon the moment of our transition.

I have previously said that a human being is exactly

the same one minute after his dissolution as he was one minute before it. That is borne out by what I have just said. It is the great difference between our real selves and the personality which we present for outward view. We are just the same in our true selves, but we may not be recognisably so. It is not so much that we have altered but that we are no longer subject to the stresses that produce the unpleasant qualities that were observable in us when we were on the earth. Remove the causes of the distempers and the latter will disappear also.

Here in spirit lands we have nothing to disturb us. On the contrary, we have everything that will bring us contentment. Our true natures thrive and expand upon such glories and splendours as the spirit world alone has to offer. We work, not for an earthly subsistence, but for the joy that comes with doing work that is both useful and congenial, and above all things, work that is of service to our fellow beings. The reward which the work brings with it is not a transient reward as is the case with so much mundane labour, but a reward that will bring us eventually to a higher state of living.

To us here in the spirit world, life is pleasure, always pleasure. We work hard, and sometimes long, but that work is pleasure to us. We have not the tiresome wearying toil that you have upon earth. We are not solitary beings fighting for our existence amid a world that can be, and so often is, somewhat indifferent to our struggles. Here in these realms wherein I live, there is not one solitary individual of whatever nationality under the sun who would not come immediately to the assistance of any one of us upon the merest glimmering of our needing help. And such help it is! There is no false pride that precludes our accepting help from a fellow creature anxious to give it.

Millions of us though there be, yet there is not one sign, not one atom of discord to be seen throughout the immense extent of these realms. Unity and concord are two of the plainest characteristics to be observed and understood and appreciated to the full.

And so you see, my good friend, there are firm grounds for not returning to visit you upon earth with exactly those characteristics by which we were so well known to you when we lived on earth. Our tempers were very often sorely tried in those days upon earth. Those times are gone now, and you know us as we really are. You did not know us for our true selves when we were with you in the flesh. That was no one's fault but own. Certainly it was not yours. We are sometimes sorry we were not outwardly of a more genial nature, but we were—and still are—but human after all, and it is upon this factor that we will all base our defence, if defence be needed. Had conditions been different with us, perhaps we should have been different, too.

When we come to the spirit world and look back upon that part of our life that we have spent on earth, we are oft-times rather shocked by the quite ridiculous importance which we placed upon some trivial incident in our daily life, an incident which caused us to appear intolerant, shall we say?—or hasty or quick tempered.

When we return to you, who are still upon earth, we do our utmost to present ourselves as we now truly are, shorn of those earthly disfigurations in our characters and temperaments by which we were perhaps too easily recognised. Such apparent change in our personality should not be so mysterious to you now, after this brief exposition. The change may seem amazing upon first acquaintance; it may even lead some of our friends to doubt our identity! It is rather pleasant to be doubted upon such a basis. At least it demonstrates to us that we have cleared ourselves of the trammels of earthly inhibitions in the full expression of our real natures.

It must not be thought, however, that we lose our individuality in this process. We retain that always. It is something which we have built up during our lives on earth, something that will characterize us and distinguish us, each from the other. We are not all reduced to an insipid uniformity. We retain our tastes and predilections; but our virtues never become as vices in their outward expression. We are healthy in body and mind, but our outlook has in so many things undergone a fundamental change.

The joy of living is a phrase of which you cannot have even the barest understanding while you are yet upon the earth-plane. It is not surprising, therefore, that we should exhibit a little of that joy when we visit you on earth. Some of us, even, dare not show ourselves to you as we really are, because some folk might be shocked! There are so many people on earth who regard us from a restricted self-conscious point of view. There would seem to be a feeling of piety in the air sometimes which we are not pleased to see when we visit you. To receive us with bated breath is not a reception according to our liking. It savours too much of the suggestion that as we have now become celestial beings (to use a favourite term), therefore we must be treated as such, that is, with gravity, with decorum, and in a manner redolent of the church sanctuary. That is not a natural environment to us. It is, in fact, thoroughly artificial, both to us and to you. We like to be just ourselves as we are, and we like you to be yourselves just as we really know you.

It is strange to us that people should look upon us as a different race of beings merely because we have gone through the process known as dying. We have simply discarded our physical body for ever, left it upon the earth, and taken up our life in another and vastly superior world. The whole process of transition which is so much feared by the folk on earth, is a natural, normal, and painless process. It is as natural and painless as removing your outer garment when you have no further use for it. The world into which we have made our entrance is a real world, solid and perpetually enduring. The people who inhabit this spirit world are real people of flesh and blood, people who once walked upon earth as you do now.

All that is great in man survives and is taken with him into this very spirit world where new avenues, far greater, finer, and broader, are for ever opening before him. There is no limit to what immense heights he can reach, whether he be scientist, or artist, or musician, or a follower of any other of the myriad worthy occupations that are to be found upon earth.

Some of us here, in these and other realms, have made many brief visits to the earth to tell our friends there something of what transpires in this great spirit world. And in doing so we have seen the shadow that hangs over so many people's lives, the shadow of 'death' and the 'grave', those two ogres that frighten so many good souls, filling them with a dread that is utterly and completely unwarranted. Man was never intended to go through his earthly life with this monstrous dark shadow for ever hanging over him. It is unnatural and thoroughly bad. It has been raised by men upon earth in remote periods of the earth's history, and it has so continued for the generality of earth's dwellers for generation after generation of the incarnate. It is but natural that, with the opportunity presenting itself, we should visit the earth, and by bringing with us a little of the light of knowledge, we should be able to dispel the fears of death of the physical body that haunts so many people, and in place of those fears to give some knowledge and information of the superb lands of the spirit world wherein we now live, and wherein you yourself will one day come to join us.

In place of fears of a speculative 'hereafter' we try to show you something of the brilliant prospect that lies before you when that happy moment arrives for you to take up your true and undoubted heritage in the spirit world.

It has been my very pleasant occupation to give you some details of this land, and I am very conscious of the many thoughts and feelings of kindness and good-will that are constantly coming to me from my friends upon earth. Your thoughts always unfailingly reach me, and each is answered, though, alas, you may be unaware of it. It is because of this inability to hear my personal and direct reciprocation of your good thoughts that I here thank you for them with all my heart. We have travelled some distance together in our discussions of life in the spirit world, although we have touched but briefly upon so vast a theme.

And so, in taking a brief leave of our subject, I will take also a brief leave of you, and in doing so I would say to you:

Benedicat te omnipotens Deus.